FOUR THOUSAND YEARS OF JEWISH HISTORY

Then and Now

Text and graphics by Jack Lefcourt

KTAV Publishing House, Inc. • Jersey City, NJ

Library of Congress Cataloging-in-Publication Data

Lefcourt, Jack.
    Four thousand years of Jewish history : then and now / by Jack Lefcourt.
        p.   cm.
    ISBN 978-1-60280-132-5
    1. Jews—History—Juvenile literature. 2.   Judaism—History—Juvenile literature. I.   Title.
    DS118.L4713   2009
    909'.04974—dc22

                    2009036558

Published by
KTAV Publishing House, Inc.
930 Newark Avenue
Jersey City, NJ 07306
Email: adam@ktav.com
www.ktav.com
(201) 963-9524
Fax (201) 963-0102

Contents

Who are the Jews? Where did we come from? When did it all begin?
Here is what we know…

Four thousand years ago (around 2000 B.C.E.), four people started out on a long journey. They were Terah, his son Abraham, Abraham's wife Sarah, and nephew Lot. They came from a city named Ur, in a kingdom called Babylonia (roughly where Iraq is today).

We do not know why they left their home. Ur was an old and once prosperous city. Babylonia was already an ancient kingdom whose best days were behind it.

Perhaps Terah sensed there was something wrong in his town. Maybe he didn't like the way people were acting. Whatever the case, he and his family packed up their belongings and left.

As they journeyed west from Ur, Terah and his companions came upon the Euphrates River, and crossed it. Upon reaching the other side, these four travelers became the first people to be identified in the bible as "Hebrews".

Why this name? "Hebrew" is an English translation for the word "Ivriim". What does "Ivriim" mean? It means roughly,…"the people from the other side of the river".

Onward the four travelers ventured to the land of Haran (where Turkey is today). It is here, we believe, that Terah's long journey came to an end. Aged, and no doubt weary from travel, the family patriarch passed on, leaving Abraham at the helm. We could imagine his fear and uncertainty at this moment.

As the bible relates, it is in Haran, following Terah's death, that Abraham first encounters Jehovah. God proposes, to the now 75-year-old Abraham, a covenant; an agreement. If Abraham and his children follow God's instructions, live by His rules, and maintain certain family practices, God will, in turn, protect them as His "Chosen people".

This encounter between God and Abraham marks the very dawn of what would come to be the Jewish religion.

The promise made by Abraham to keep God's covenant was passed on to Abraham's son Isaac, Isaac's son Jacob, Jacob's sons, and so on. For the next few hundred years, the descendants of Abraham inhabited the land of Canaan (where Israel and Palestine are today), practicing the laws of their faith, and keeping their promise to God.

Around 1600 B.C.E., a great famine swept the land of Canaan, forcing the descendants of Abraham to seek a new home. Eventually, they made their way to Egypt. At this time, Egypt was governed by a group of people called the Hyksos. They were, in some ways, distant cousins. Like the Hebrews, the Hyksos were a Semitic tribe from the east. Possibly for this reason, they welcomed the Hebrews into their land, showing them warmth and respect.

Within a hundred years however, the Hyksos were overthrown. The new rulers of Egypt were not so friendly. They oppressed and enslaved many, including the Hebrews, the Hyksos, and others. For the next few centuries, Abraham's descendants toiled as slaves under the pharaohs of Egypt.

How did the Hebrews survive this period of enslavement intact? What kept them together as a distinct people? History books tell us little about their experience in Egypt. What the bible does tell us is this: The descendants of Abraham who had entered Egypt during the Hyksos reign exited some four hundred years later as the "Israelites". Their destination: Canaan.

A dream to return to their ancestral homeland: This, we believe, was the common thread of memory and hope, which served to keep the Hebrew people together in bondage.

In the coming chapters, we will learn about the role of Moses and Joshua in leading the Israelites back to the land of Canaan, and the rise of the Israelite kingdom under Saul, David, and Solomon. And, we will follow the journey of Abraham's descendants through the various cultures of the ancient world.

In chapter one, we finished by posing the question: How did the Hebrews remain together as an intact group of people during their four hundred year ordeal in Egypt? There is no certain answer here. Practices of the early Hebrews may have been maintained in isolation by some of those enslaved. Possibly their longing for freedom and a return to the land of Canaan would have given the descendants of Abraham common purpose and direction.

Around 1200 B.C.E., a set of circumstances arose which set free the Israelites (the Hebrews) from bondage, and served to strengthen their identity as a distinct people. Central to these events was a man named Moses.

Who was Moses? We understand him to have been of Hebrew origin, but born and bred into Egyptian life and traditions. Raised as royalty, Moses would not have been subjected to the treatment his Hebrew brethren experienced in the same land. And yet, a bond remained.

Moses with the Tablets, by Rembrandt Van Rijn, 1659

We are familiar with the story of his witnessing the beating of a Hebrew slave, and the fury that welled up inside him upon seeing this. We know of the murder he committed in rage, and his following exile in Sinai.

As the bible tells, it was in Sinai, in the town of Horeb, where Moses first hears the voice of God. Emanating from a burning bush, the voice tells Moses:

"Come now therefore, and I will send you unto Pharaoh, that you may bring forth My people the children of Israel out of Egypt." (Exodus 3:9-10)

Eight hundred years earlier, a man named Abraham had heard this same voice. Now it was Moses' turn!

The uprising and exodus of the Israelites under Moses is believed to have taken place during the reign of King Ramses the second, placing it around 1200 B.C.E.. The details of this event are debated and discussed to this day. How many Israelites followed Moses across the desert? How do we account for the parting of the Red Sea, allowing Moses' followers to escape the armies of Pharaoh? These are valid questions.

What is certain is this: The role of Moses in the continuation of the Hebrew/Israelite people was a great one. He inspired them to revolt against their oppressors, led them out of Egypt, and introduced a new element to their society: The Ten Commandments.

A set of written laws to be remembered and obeyed would, from this point forward, act as the "glue" which kept the Israelites (in time, the Jewish people) together, wherever they went, and whoever they lived among.

After forty years of wandering, the Hebrews, now "the Children of Israel", finally arrived in the land of their distant ancestors. Moses had passed on, and a new generation of his followers had replaced the old. It was under Joshua, Moses' successor, that the Israelites walked forward into the "Promised Land".

It was a difficult entry. The land was inhabited by various Canaanite tribes, some of whom were the distant descendants of Abraham who had not made the journey to Egypt four hundred years earlier. Instead, they had stayed behind. How would local Canaanites accept these Israelite newcomers? Would they be viewed as enemies, or long-lost cousins?

The conquering of this land by Moses' followers was not peaceful. But over the following hundred years, a slow, steady integration took place. A once nomadic people, made up of many tribes, transformed into a single complex society, and cities were born. With the growth of this new culture came the need for organization. Who would govern this new country, set its laws, collect its taxes, and keep peace and order?

By 1100 B.C.E., there emerged an early system of Israelite government. It was called the Shoftim. Made up of twelve "Judges", each representing one of the twelve tribes of Israel, the

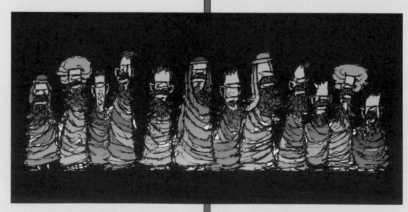

Shoftim maintained religious laws and practices throughout the land. For over a century, The Shoftim reigned. For this reason, this period is called "the Age of Judges".

It wasn't a perfect system. The Judges tended to favor the interests of their own tribes. Sometimes there were quarrels that could not be resolved. It became clear that an even stronger central power was needed. Israel now looked for a king.

Around 1000 B.C.E., "The United Kingdom of Israel" was born. It was to last for almost a century. The first anointed king of this new monarchy was a man named Saul, whose reign endured for twenty years. While he may have been first to officially sit in the throne, it is often said that Saul was a king in title only. The honor of "First King of Israel" we more often attribute to Saul's successor, David. It is with the reign of David, the "poet king", that we begin our next chapter.

Saul was a moody king. To lift his spirits, the royal court was often host to musicians and poets. Of the many minstrels who came to soothe and entertain him, one stood out as Saul's favorite. He was a young shepherd named David.

David's position in the court of King Saul grew with his reputation. Beyond his abilities with the harp, David demonstrated great courage in his toppling of a giant Philistine soldier named Goliath of Gath.

Statue of King David, by F.A. Jerichau, 1860

As a young man, David continued to impress the king. He triumphed in battle, and in time, was made commander of Saul's troops. In many ways, David became like a son to Saul. And yet, in his later years, Saul came to fear David, seeing him as a threat to his power.

History shows that kings are often jealous people, suspicious of those around them. For all of David's bravery, service, and devotion to his kingdom and its leader, Saul's worries only grew. The aging king came to believe that David might rise up, and one day replace him as ruler. He was right!!!

In his homeland of Judah (south of Israel), far from the jealous tantrums of Saul. David found he had many admirers. There, he quickly rose to power, and became king of the region. Upon Saul's death, David returned to Israel, the kingdom of the north, with legions of his followers, and took command of the royal court. David now ruled two kingdoms: Israel and Judah. His reign would last close to forty years, and his accomplishments would be many.

We recall from chapter two the forming of the "United Kingdom of Israel". It was under David's leadership that this union took place. Israel and Judah were now one state. Through conquest, David's United Kingdom grew, becoming five times the size of Israel today. The new king made Jerusalem its capital. There, he made plans to build a Holy Temple. Over David's forty-year rule, Israel became quite an empire, commanding many armies, and engaging in trade with many nations.

Among later generations of Jews, there emerged a great longing for a "messiah": a leader who would restore the Kingdom of Israel to glory. It was with the image of David in mind that this dream took hold.

Following the death of David, the United Kingdom welcomed a new leader: David's son, Solomon. Where David's rule was marked by war and expansion, the period of Solomon's reign was one of peace and prosperity. It is said he was a wise and just king, skilled at solving disputes. Like his father, Solomon ruled for forty years. During this time, many of the great plans made by David were seen through to completion, including the building of the Holy Temple in Jerusalem.

Under Solomon, Israel became an industrial nation. Shipping and trade replaced agriculture as its main form of livelihood, and great wealth was produced. But, as the fortunes of the kingdom grew, so too did the quarrels between Israel and Judah. Like David before him, Solomon was from Judah, to the south. The Israelites came to resent their "foreign" king, and the heavy taxes he placed on them. In time, disagreements between the two regions became so great, even Solomon, for all his wisdom, could not patch things up.

Upon Solomon's death, the "glue" which held the two kingdoms together as one came undone. Solomon's son, Rehoboam, became ruler of Judah. But, his authority was not recognized north of his homeland. Instead, Israel picked its own leader, Jeroboam. For the next hundred years, the two kingdoms squabbled and bickered, and did not notice, all the while, the growing threat of invasion from nations that surrounded them.

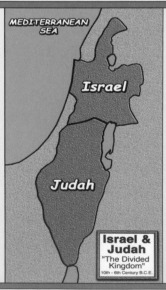

MEDITERRANEAN SEA

Israel

Judah

Israel & Judah
"The Divided Kingdom"
10th - 6th Century B.C.E.

A divided kingdom is far more vulnerable, and easily attacked, than one which is united. Over the following few centuries, the inhabitants of Judah and Israel would learn this lesson well. Both kingdoms found themselves repeatedly at war with neighboring powers. From the north, Assyria invaded Israel, leading to its downfall in 722 B.C.E. From the east, Babylonia attacked Judah, and conquered its armies in 586 B.C.E. In four hundred years, from the time of King David to the Babylonian takeover of Judah, a nation had risen, expanded, divided, and collapsed.

Judaica Crossword Puzzle 1

Down

1. Ur was a city in this ancient kingdom. (Chapter 1)
2. The place where Abraham first spoke with God. (Chapter 1)
3. Abraham and his family crossed this river. (Chapter 1)
4. He guided the Israelites from Egypt in 1200 B.C.E. (Chapter 2)
5. Where Moses saw the burning bush. (Chapter 2)
6. The kingdom north of Judah. (Chapter 3)
7. The kingdom south of Israel. (Chapter 3)
8. He was the first king of Israel, and quite moody. (Chapters 2 and 3)
9. Abraham's wife. (Chapter 1)
10. A group of twelve judges. (Chapter 2)
11. Abraham's nephew. (Chapter 1)
12. Solomon's son. (Chapter 3)
13. This musical king united Judah and Israel. (Chapter 3)
14. This nation conquered Israel in 722 B.C.E. (Chapter 3)
15. The agreement between God and Abraham. (Chapter 1)
16. The region where Moses lived in exile. (Chapter 2)

Across

1. He first spoke with God in Haran. (Chapter 1)
2. The Babylonian city where Abraham came from. (Chapter 1)
3. He wore a coat of many colors. (This is not in the text! Do you know the answer?)
4. Abraham's father. (Chapter 1)
5. These people ruled Egypt when the Hebrews arrived. (Chapter 1)
6. The Hebrews left this place around 1200 B.C.E. (Chapters 1 and 2)
7. Moses did not make it to the Promised Land, but this guy did. (Chapter 2)
8. David's son. (Chapter 3)
9. The Shoftim ruled during the Age of _____. (Chapter 2)
10. Moses and the Israelites crossed what sea? (Chapter 2)
11. For four hundred years, Abraham's descendants lived here, before going to Egypt. (Chapter 1)
12. It means "the people from the other side of the river." (Chapter 1)
13. People who live "on the move" are called what? (Chapter 2)
14. The Philistine giant David slew with a slingshot. (Chapter 3)

12

We have witnessed the emergence, over fifteen hundred years, of a group of people called the Hebrews. Starting with Abraham around 2000 B.C.E., to the fall of Judah in 586 B.C.E, we have seen a family become an extended tribe, and that tribe become a nation, and ultimately, a kingdom.

But what about religion? What ideas, practices, and views of the world were forming among these people over this time? When did Judaism truly begin?

From early Hebrew and Israelite practices, the Jewish religion evolved in stages. Key to this evolution were the Ten Commandments delivered by Moses at Mount Sinai. The stone tablets he bore introduced written law to the Israelites. They outlined the governing principles and basic rules of living for generations to come. Central to these principles was the revolutionary belief that God is both singular, and invisible.

This theme of an invisible god is illustrated in the story of the Golden Calf, in the book of Exodus. While roaming the Sinai Desert, following their escape from Egypt, the Israelites become desperate and lost. They had left enslavement behind, but were headed for

an uncertain future. On the windy, desolate dunes, they no doubt felt a great need for a sense of closeness to God. And so, they built statues: gods which they could see. Moses, however, was furious, and commanded his followers to destroy these idols. Why?

A god which one can see and touch is also a god which one can toy with, or throw away. As well, it can be toppled easily by others. An invisible god, however, is something different. How does one hide from such a god? A divine being we cannot see is quite a powerful force! While temples and

statues may crumble, an invisible god is unshakeable. And nowhere can one escape its ever-seeing eye! In place of earthly idols, Moses helped bring about a much grander notion of God: one universal power that cannot be destroyed.

When we consider Moses, never do we refer to him as a divine being. Rather, we see him simply as a man. God, we say, led the Israelites from Egypt. Moses was merely the instrument of God's will. In looking at things this way, we ourselves follow Moses' example. If we were to make a god out of the image of Moses, would we not be like the ancient Israelites molding a golden calf?

This simple, elegant idea of God as one invisible force became the foundation of the Jewish religion. The Ten Commandments handed by Moses to the Israelites became its first written laws. These laws, etched on stone tablets, were placed in a

I'M WATCHING YOU!

special Ark, and carried by Joshua and the Israelites into the Promised Land. Throughout Canaan it traveled, finding a permanent home in the Holy Temple in Jerusalem, during the reign of King Solomon.

The Ark of the Covenant held the first Torah. Its contents were the first written religious codes, not just for the Jews, but, so far as we know, of any people in history up to that point.

The Mosaic Laws, contained in the Ark of the Covenant, represented a great ideal. They would shape the future growth of Judaism, and have an enormous effect on other religions as well. But, the conflict between Invisible God, on the one hand, and the very human need to worship idols, on the other, did not end when the Israelites entered the Promised Land. During

the time of Kings David and Solomon, Judaism had very little to do with the study of ideas. There was no published Torah, as yet, for Jews to keep and read in their homes. The Temple was run by a priesthood, and religious practice consisted mostly of ritual sacrifice, made in the form of burnt offerings.

Idol worship became widespread throughout the kingdom. Perhaps people had a great need to feel connected with God, not just at the Temple, but in their own homes. And so, a whole array of "golden calves" appeared.

The kings of Israel and Judah spent much energy building the nation and expanding its trade routes. All the while, little attention was paid to the dangers that idolatry posed. Priests ran the Temple, citizens brought their offerings, and in this fashion the religion pretty much "coasted along". As the Jewish nation became

imperiled by growing forces that surrounded it, so too, the fledgling Jewish religion found itself at risk.

In the latter phase of the kingdoms, before they fell to Assyria and Babylonia, a new voice came to be heard among the people of Israel and Judah: that of the Prophets.

Adoration of the Golden Calf, by Nicolas Poussin, 1635

Throughout history, there have always been those who could see past the comforts of the moment. The Prophets warned of dangers, not just from outside the kingdom walls, but within the spiritual life of the nation as well. A return to idolatry, many of them argued, was just the beginning of a coming darkness.

To many, these Prophets seemed like "crack-pots" looking to stir up trouble. Conflicts arose between them and the Temple priests. In later years, however, as the Jews were once again carted off into captivity in different lands, the words of Prophets like Amos, Isaiah, Jeremiah, and others would come to have greater meaning. And their ideas would continue to echo, breathing new life into the Jewish faith.

"For I desire righteousness, not sacrifice, and knowledge of God more than burnt offerings." Hosea 6:6

"It has been told to you, O man, what is good, and what the Lord does require of you: Only to do justly, and to love mercy, and to walk humbly with your God." Micah 6:8

"Their land also is full of idols; Everyone worships the work of his own hands, that which his own fingers have made." Isaiah 2:8

These words were spoken in the eighth century B.C.E., by the Prophets Hosea, Micah, and Isaiah.

Who were the Prophets? By trade, they were herdsmen, scribes, teachers, tutors to kings, and rebel priests. Their collective accomplishment would be the reinvention of Judaism.

In the last chapter, we saw the emergence of the Prophets sometime shortly before Israel's fall to Assyria. At the time that they preached, few listened. They were the laughing stocks of many. And yet, looking back in later years, their words came to be understood as warning signals to a sleeping nation.

The three Prophets quoted above were among the earliest of their kind. They saw, well in advance, the dangers that idol worship posed. They saw the future fall of their kingdom as divine punishment for sin. They condemned the worship of man over the worship of God. They argued that good deeds and righteous behavior had far greater value than the rituals of the Temple. And, they sought to prepare the Jews for survival in dark times ahead.

When Assyria conquered Israel, the people of Judah shuddered. They knew at once that the world around them was not so stable as they had thought. Their neighbors to the north, after repeated attempts to hold off invasion, were finally overwhelmed. They were taken away into captivity in a foreign land, and forced to leave all that was familiar to them

behind. Would Judah suffer the same fate? Indeed, a century and a half later, it would. But, during the time in between, great changes took place in the southern kingdom which helped ensure the future survival of the Jewish faith. Central to these changes was a great king named Josiah.

Josiah became King of Judah in 638 B.C.E. By this time, Prophetic writings of a century earlier were starting to be taken seriously, and this change in attitude was reflected in many of Josiah's initiatives. He brought about social reforms to make Judah a fairer, more just place to live for its inhabitants. Religious idols were outlawed. And written codes of ethics came to assume a larger role in the conduct of Judean society.

Josiah took great interest in a scroll of ancient Israelite origin, unearthed in the Temple by his High Priest Hilkiah, bearing passages he believed to have been written in the time of Moses and Joshua.

The scroll was, in fact, an early book of law. Today many scholars believe some of the writings contained in the scroll ultimately found their way into the Book of Deuteronomy, several centuries later.

Whatever the case, it is clear that the finding, and subsequent presentation of this text by Josiah to the people of Jerusalem marks and important, early phase in the evolution of the Jewish Torah.

In short, Judaism was moving away from priests and ancient Temple practices. It was becoming a book. Ideas, laws and justice were assuming greater importance than sacrifice and ritual. As well, Judaism was becoming something people could carry with them. Religion was now portable!

When Judah fell to Babylonia in 586 B.C.E., its inhabitants went into captivity. Their Temple in Jerusalem was destroyed, and they were forced to leave behind their homes and livelihoods. But their experience in exile would be quite different from that of the Israelites. Unlike the people of Israel, now captive in Assyria, the former citizens of Judah had

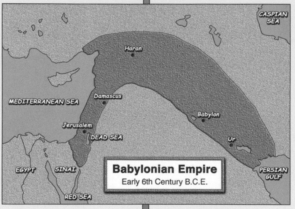

Babylonian Empire
Early 6th Century B.C.E.

something to take with them; a portable religion. No longer dependant on idols or their Temple, they now had a book of written laws to bond around. And, there were other factors which enabled them to maintain their identity.

Around 539 B.C.E., Babylonia itself was conquered by an even more powerful nation to the north: Persia. Unlike the Assyrians and Babylonians, the Persians were a comparatively tolerant people. They were not interested in crushing those who they held in captivity.

Prophet Isaiah, detail from the Sistene Chapel, by Michelangelo, 1509

They allowed, even encouraged, the continued religious practices of foreign peoples among them. In Assyria, the people of Israel lost their nation, religion, and identity. At this point, their lineage vanishes from the pages of history. But in Persian-occupied Babylonia, the people of Judah stayed intact.

Jeremiah Lamenting the Destruction of Jerusalem, by Rembrandt Van Rijn, 1630

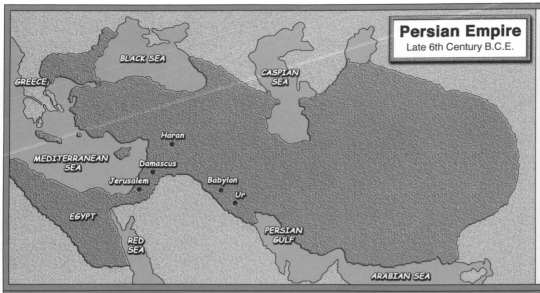

Persian Empire
Late 6th Century B.C.E.

GREECE

BLACK SEA

CASPIAN SEA

MEDITERRANEAN SEA

Haran

Damascus

Jerusalem

Babylon

Ur

EGYPT

RED SEA

PERSIAN GULF

ARABIAN SEA

The Persian Empire of the sixth century B.C.E., was huge. At its peak, it would encompass the lands we now call Turkey, Syria, Lebanon, Israel, Egypt, Iraq, Iran, Libya, Pakistan, and Afghanistan.

Jews living in this vast region during the sixth and fifth centuries B.C.E., were of conflicting minds. Many welcomed the opportunities this great cosmopolitan culture offered, and sought to assimilate completely, leaving all traces of their Jewish past behind. Some wanted to stay, yet maintain their religious identity. Others still longed to return to Judah and see the restoration of their former nation to glory.

These competing attitudes are expressed in the words of Prophets of the era. Jeremiah, on the one hand, preached survival of Jewish tradition through education:

"Build houses and dwell in them; and plant gardents, and eat the fruit of them...that you may be increased there and not diminished. And seek the peace of the city where I have caused you to be

carried away captives."
Jeremiah 29:8-9

Ezekiel, on the other hand, urged Jews to return to the land of Palestine:

"I will gather you from the peoples and assemble you out of the countries among which you have been scattered, and I will give you the land of Israel."
Ezekiel 11:17

21

This conflict between the urge to assimilate, and the need for identity, has remained a theme of Jewish existence throughout history. Miraculously, both were accomplished by the Jews of Babylonia. They lived and prospered in their new environment, and at the same time, stayed intact as a religious entity. How? By adaptation.

The Jews in Babylonian exile no longer had their Temple. They did, however, have with them a book of laws, a legacy of the reconstructive efforts of King Josiah. Jews would gather regularly in small groups to share and discuss the scriptures. They did so in modest assembly houses, which, in time, sprouted up all over Babylonia and elsewhere in Persia.

Humble in comparison to the Holy Temple of Jerusalem, these houses served the purpose of giving continued location and focus to the scattered Jewish populations in exiles. The Greek word for "assembly" is "synagogue." And, it was by this term that these houses came to be known in centuries to come.

As mentioned earlier, there were many Jews who longed to return to Judah, and there rebuild their former kingdom. King Cyrus of Persia sympathized with their cause, and late in the sixth century B.C.E., opened the gates of freedom, allowing Jews under his domain to return, once again, to Palestine. He even helped finance the construction of a second Holy Temple in Jerusalem, completed in 515 B.C.E.

But Judah, by this time, was in ruin. Farm fields, once flush with crops, lay fallow. And the Jewish religion, once the binding force of the region, was but a memory to the few who still lived there. A great reconstruction, both spiritual and structural, was called for.

During the fifth century B.C.E., many Jews did return to Palestine. Along with the Temple in Jerusalem, communities were rebuilt. Never again, though, would there be a "Kingdom" of Judah or Israel on the same scale as before. From this point

forward, the region would remain, more or less, a "province" of other powers. But where Jewish nationhood failed to achieve its former glory, the Jewish religion continued its great evolution.

In 444 B.C.E., the Five Books of Moses, Genesis, Exodus, Leviticus, Numbers and Deuteronomy, were assembled under the collective title, "the Pentateuch." Compiled in Babylonia, the books made their way to Palestine sometime early in the fourth century B.C.E.

They were presented to the people there by Nehemiah, the Persian-appointed governor of Judah, and by a Priest named Ezra. The Jewish Torah, as we know it today, was born!

But who could read it? By this time, very few people understood Hebrew. Aramaic, a mixture of various middle-eastern and Persian dialects, was the dominant language of the empire. It was the "English" of it time. The Pentateuch needed interpreters. And so, a school developed, called the Midrash. Here, Jews could listen to the scriptures in a language familiar to them. Those who guided their learning were, in some ways, the first rabbis.

As well, a regular schedule of readings was instituted. Nehemiah, the Persian appointed governor of Judah, and Ezra, a priest and scholar, decreed that the Pentateuch would be read from every Sabbath, and twice during the week, to ensure its continual place in the lives of Jews throughout Palestine. The Mosaic Laws were to be understood by all.

When Persia fell to Macedonia and Greece in the fourth century B.C.E., the Jews of Palestine, once again, found themselves governed by new and strange foreign powers. But the basic institutions of their religion were now in place. The Five Books of Moses, the Synagogue and Midrash, and a tradition of weekly Torah readings would sustain the Jewish people through all that lay ahead.

Judaica Timeline Activity

This Judaica Timeline represents, from left to right, the first sixteen hundred years of Jewish history. Listed below are ten key events or periods discussed in chapters one through seven. See if you can place these events in proper sequence in the numbered timeline boxes!

1. Moses leads the Israelites from Egypt
2. Babylonia conquers Judah
3. The United Kingdom of Israel begins
4. The Hebrews go to Egypt
5. Presentation of the Pentateuch by Nehemiah and Ezra
6. Abraham crosses the Euphrates River
7. Assyria conquers Israel
8. Slavery in Egypt
9. Abraham's children live in Canaan
10. The United Kingdom of Israel ends

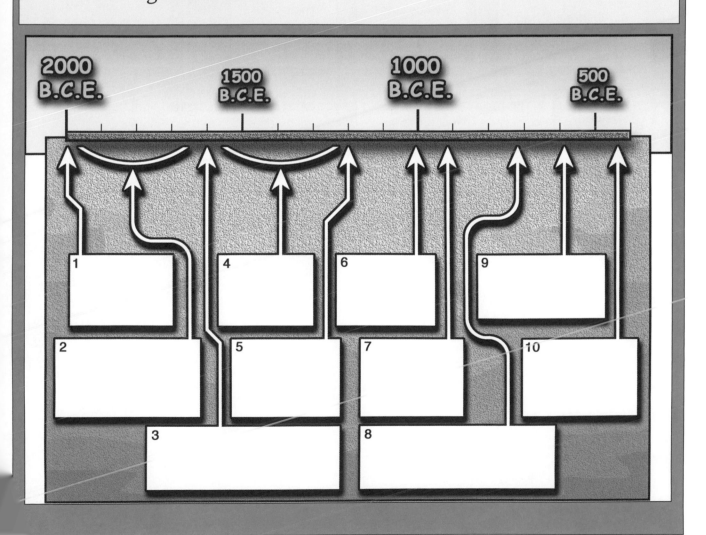

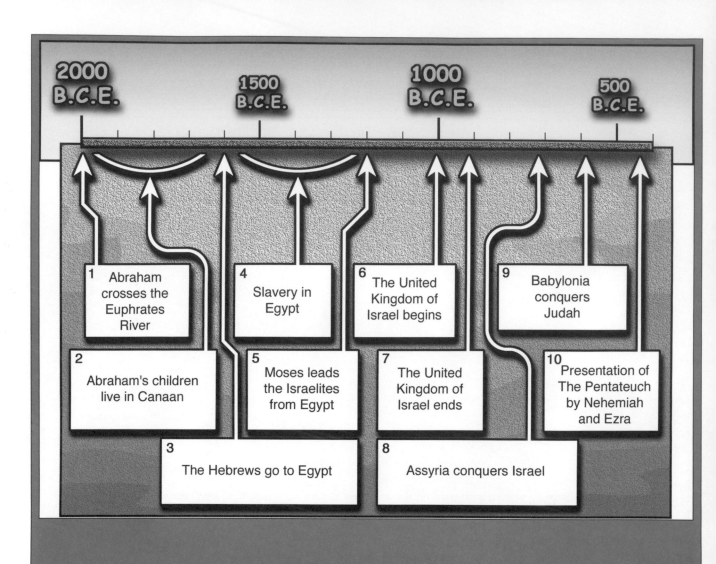

Assimilation versus identity. Idolatry versus spirituality.

These two themes, as we have seen, are central to understanding the course of Jewish history in the ancient world. In Babylonian exile, the people of Judah struggled greatly to maintain their religious identity. The Torah, the emergence of the synagogue, and the making of a portable religion were all innovations that helped them in this effort. But in the centuries that followed, pressures to assimilate would only become greater. As Persia teetered, and finally tumbled in the fourth century B.C.E., the Jews of Palestine found themselves under the influence of a new, emerging force in the world: Greece.

Who were the Greeks? Let's backtrack a little. In the eighth century B.C.E., around the time Israel was being invaded by Assyria, a small cluster of city-states were forming in the northern Mediterranean: Athens, Sparta, and Corinth. These communities made up the foundation of what would become the Greek Empire. Over the next few hundred years, as Greece grew in influence

and military might, it challenged the various kingdoms to the east and south. Even as Persia rose to dominance under King Cyrus, it found itself threatened by this new, upstart western power. In 334 B.C.E., under the leadership of Alexander the Great, the armies of Greece defeated mighty Persia once and for all. Palestine was now under new foreign rule.

At first, the Jews welcomed Alexander and the Greeks. There was no attempt made by this new invading force to hold its subjects captive. A "live and let live" attitude prevailed. So long as the Jews of Palestine paid their taxes, their lives and customs would remain undisturbed.

There were many things the Jews liked about the Greeks. They were a scholarly, educated people. Greek philosophy and poetry became popular. And the Greek theatre offered a new, fascinating forum for entertainment. In turn, many Greeks saw the Jews as an elevated, learned people, devoted to ideas and intelligent discussion. And between the two cultures, great exchanges of intellect took place.

But there were also divisions. To many Jews at the time, Greek society seemed to lack a moral compass. The Mosaic concept of a singular, invisible God stood at odds with contemporary Greek thinking. And to many Greeks, the Jews often appeared as prudes, unwilling to participate in Greek social affairs.

The spirit of Greek culture had a name: "Hellenism". And it was the mission of Greek authorities to "Hellenize" all foreign peoples in their midst. What did this mean? In short, those living under Greek rule were to speak, dress, and act Greek. To many Jews, this did not pose a problem. After all, in the past, becoming Babylonian or Persian in appearance had not stopped them from being Jewish.

But "Hellenism", in many ways, also amounted to a corruption of things sacred to Jews. The Greeks promoted sporting events on Temple grounds. They enforced the universal worship of Greek gods, and encouraged Jews to embrace a Greek lifestyle.

Where, at first, the Greeks had appeared tolerant and willing to allow Jewish religious identity to remain intact, in time it became clear this was not the case. Statues of Zeus popped up everywhere, even in the Jewish Temple. Like modern billboards, Greek images cluttered the streets of Jerusalem. Through Hellenism, idol worship was returning to Palestine.

Like the Prophets of centuries earlier, there were some Jews who started to see the dangers. These "anti-Hellenizers" sought to keep Jewish religious institutions free of Greek influence. They formed a political party, the Hasideans (not to be confused with the Hasidic movement of many centuries later), and began, bit by bit, to rebel against the Greek world around them. Great conflicts arose, not so much between Jews and Greeks, but rather, between pro-Hellenic Jews and the Hasideans. In time, things got violent. Priests adorned in Greek garb were tossed from the Temple, and Greek statues were smashed on the streets below.

As troubles in Palestine brewed, the Greek authorities took notice, and quickly got annoyed. Greek soldiers were sent in to keep the peace, but found waiting for them an armed resistance they hadn't anticipated. Increasingly the Greeks had to devote more of their military resources to dealing with the Jews of Palestine. Jerusalem came under military occupation, and Jews of all persuasions found themselves besieged in their own city.

The story of the Maccabee revolt stems from this period. In a small suburb of Jerusalem, an anti-Hellenic priest named Mattathias murdered a Greek official, rather than be forced to make sacrifice to a statue of Zeus. In response, Greek-led Syrian troops were sent in to make arrests. But the Hasidean movement, at this point, had become much

stronger than the Greeks knew. Mattathias' sons had organized a well-armed militia called the Maccabees ("the Hammers"). They were, in effect, the military wing of the Hasidean party. When the soldiers arrived in Jerusalem to arrest Mattathias and others, the Maccabees attacked, and pursued them right out of the city.

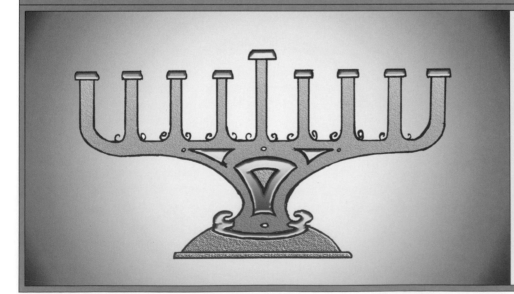

Every year, when we light the Menorah during Hanukkah, we commemorate the victory of the Maccabees, and the retaking of the Temple of Jerusalem.

Following the Maccabee revolt of 164 B.C.E., fighting between the armies of Greece and the Hasidean Jews of Palestine continued for over twenty years. The conflict was complicated. Many Jews enjoyed living in a Greek world, and did not see their Hellenic rulers as enemies. Many Greeks did not object to Jewish home rule of Judah, and

couldn't see the point in continued occupation. Gradually, the Greeks withdrew. They pulled out their troops, and allowed Judah its independence. In 143 B.C.E., the distant descendants of Abraham, the followers of Moses, and heirs to King David, once again, had a kingdom.

Hasmonean Kingdom
1st Century B.C.E.

It would last only about seventy-six years. The Hasmonean Dynasty it was called, named for the priestly family of Mattathias. Few recorded heroes come from this period. It was a kingdom made weak from political infighting and bickering. Its first leader was Simon, the only surviving son of Mattathias. He was said to be wise and shrewd. But very quickly into his rule, he made a questionable move, one that helped seal his own kingdom's fate less than a century later.

There is an old saying, which goes: "The enemy of my enemy is my friend." The Hasmonean leaders saw that Greece had an enemy, a rival power to the west called Rome. Simon figured that if Rome had an ally in the new Hasmonean Kingdom, Romans in turn would defend Judah against the Greeks if need should arise. And so, a pact was made, one that ensured that Greece would never again occupy Palestine.

But, there is another old saying, which goes: "He who rides the back of a tiger winds up inside." Rome was an expanding republic at the time Greece was at its peak. It eyed the Greek domains with envy, and imagined itself the future ruling power of the region. Over the course of the first century B.C.E., Rome did in fact conquer Greece, taking its territories. But in doing so, it inherited many Greek headaches. Shaky relations with Judah, once the concern of Greece, was now a Roman problem.

No longer in need of an alliance with Judah against Greece, Rome quickly came to view the Jewish kingdom as territory to be conquered. In 63 B.C.E., the Jews of Palestine found themselves, once again, without an independent kingdom, and deep inside the belly of the "Roman tiger."

Bust of Julius Caesar, Dictator of Rome from 48 to 44 B.C.E., unknown artist

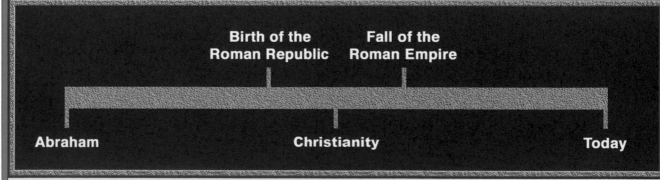

The rise and fall of the Roman Empire, the birth of Christianity, and the Diaspora, together, represent a critical phase in world history, and in the Jewish experience. These events took place across a period roughly two thousand years after Abraham, and two thousand years before today. They mark the half-way point of our journey!

The next few chapters will focus more specifically on this important period. But first, let us take a closer look at life in the Hasmonean Kingdom.

In the period building up to the Roman takeover of Judah, Judaism was in a fractured state. Conflicts between pro and anti-Greek factions had only become greater. The differing attitudes, which Jews had about their Hellenic surroundings led to the formation of three rival political parties: the Sadducees, the Pharisees, and the Essenes. Each group was a reflection of a different attitude towards Jewish identity, and to the issue of cultural assimilation.

The Essenes were a branch of the Hasideans. They rejected Greek Hellenic culture completely, seeing it in moral ruin. They felt their Mosaic traditions were in great peril. And, rather than dwell among idol worshippers, the Essenes lived in remote encampments in the outback of Palestine.

Essene

Pharisee

The Pharisees were also Hasideans. But, unlike the Essenes, they did not feel the need to remove themselves entirely from their Hellenic environment. The Pharisees were more the mainstream of Jewish spiritual life, where traditions of the synagogue and Temple met.

The Sadducees were a different bunch altogether. They embraced Greco-Roman culture, and prospered in it. They held positions of power in business and politics. They were also the last of the "Temple Jews", before the synagogue took over completely as the central institution of Jewish worship. This last point is an important one. For several hundred years, there were really two Jewish religions. There was the portable Judaism of the Prophets, of the synagogue, and Mosaic Law, spawned in the period of Babylonian exile. But there remained, still, a more ancient branch of proto-Judaism based on ritual sacrifice, and the centrality of the priest-run Temple in Jerusalem. The Sadducees were the last Temple "holdouts."

Sadducee

The Sadducees may have been open to the influence of Greek culture, but the doors of their Temple were shut. Disinclined to invite newcomers to the religion, they did not venture outside the Temple to preach. Theirs was a "members-only" club.

The Pharisees saw themselves as keepers of a "people's religion." They read from the Torah, and taught the Mosaic Laws. Their religion was less concerned with rituals of the Temple, focusing more on laws, justice, and prayer. It is from the Pharisee branch that all modern Judaism stems.

The Essenes, like the Pharisees, were followers of Moses. They believed in the written word only, and had no use for a priest-run central authority. As well, they sought to spread their religion, introducing it to peoples far and wide.

It was in a remote region of Judah, called Galilee, that a young Essene Jew named Jesus Christ preached the teachings of Moses less than a century later. And, it was the Essene sect which would give rise to a spiritual revolution that, in time, came to dominate the Roman Empire. In the coming chapters, we will continue to explore this "fork in the road" of Jewish history.

Bust of Augustus Caesar, Emperor of Rome from 23 B.C.E. to 14 C.E., unknown artist

The last century B.C.E., was an eventful time for those living under Roman rule. No sooner had it conquered Greece, and taken over Palestine, Rome itself broke out in civil war. For a time, the great republic went leaderless, as competing generals fought for command. In 48 B.C.E., Julius Caesar became supreme dictator of Rome, marking the end of the republic and the dawn of the new Roman Empire. A few decades later, its first official emperor, Augustus Caesar, was crowned.

Throughout Palestine during this time, Rome's presence was greatly felt. East of Judea (as Judah was now called by the Romans), lay Parthia, a remnant of the former Persian Empire. To keep guard against this possible foe, Roman fighting units were stationed all over Palestine.

They found, however, they were not entirely welcome. Just as the Hasideans, a century earlier, had rebelled against Greek authority, many Jews now attempted to push the Romans out, and reclaim their kingdom.

Over the following century, into the Common Era (C.E.), a series of Jewish uprisings occupied much of Rome's energies. Rome appointed "procurators" to preside over Judea, and keep order among the rebellious factions. Revolts against these imposed leaders led to full-scale wars against the Roman legions. Three Judean/Roman wars were fought between 65 and 135 C.E. In each case, the Romans were held back by the Judean armies, and forced to retreat. It was Rome's superior numbers, in the end, which led them to final victory.

In 135 C.E., Judah fell, once and for all, to mighty Rome. Emperor Hadrian then banished all Jews from the land of Palestine. Some, captives of the war, were sold into slavery. Many went east, to Parthia. Most, in time, became citizens of Rome, which they were first allowed to do in 212. This banishment marks the onset of what has come to be known in Jewish history as the Diaspora. It is a Greek term meaning "scattering." From this point forward, Jews would find themselves scattered among many nations, and assimilating into many cultures. It would not be for another two thousand years, with the establishing of modern-day Israel, that Jews would, once again, claim nationhood in Palestine.

How did Judaism remain a religion and culture in the long age of Diaspora? What innovations kept Jews together while being scattered so far apart?

Jews in Babylonian exile, we recall, developed a portable religion. They kept intact by adapting to new surroundings. Synagogues replaced the Temple. Prayer replaced sacrifice. And the community was bound to a common set of laws.

For rabbis in these exile communities, it was difficult to know how exactly to "keep things kosher." Circumstances made it difficult often to follow certain laws. And so, a kind of "guide book" was slowly compiled over time. Its purpose was to give further instruction to Jews in exile on how to continue observing Mosaic Law. The book allowed for versatility. Jews in different lands could practice their religion in slightly different ways, and still "be Jewish."

Many rabbis and scholars contributed to the book. They did so for centuries by oral tradition. That is, by word of mouth. In time, their many guidelines were written, and collected in a book: The Talmud. For Jews of the Diaspora, this new companion book to the Torah was the key. It would ensure the future survival of Judaism.

There is a strange, wonderful story from the first century C.E., involving a rabbi, a Roman general, and a coffin...

In 68 C.E., Rome and Judea had been at war for three years. Vespasian, the Roman general, had captured Judea, but not Jerusalem. Rather than continue fighting, Vespasian lay siege on the city, hoping to starve its inhabitants into surrender. At this time, in Jerusalem, there lived a rabbi named Jochanan Ben Zakkai. The rabbi foresaw the future victory of Rome and the tragic scattering of his people. He decided that he needed to meet with Vespasian.

Bust of Vespasian, Emperor of Rome from 69 to 79 C.E., unknown artist

To leave the city under military siege would be difficult, though. And so, Ben Zakkai came up with a curious plan. He would fake his own death. Carrying their rabbi in a coffin, Ben Zakkai's disciples were granted permission to leave Jerusalem for burial purposes. The rabbi was then carried to the Roman encampments, and to the tent of Vespasian.

The general was, no doubt, surprised to see this elderly man pop out of the wooden box. After introducing himself, the rabbi then said to Vespasian: "I have two things to tell you. One is a prophecy, the other, a request." Ben Zakkai prophesied that Vespasian would soon become Emperor

of Rome. Liking what he heard, the general told the rabbi to continue. The request was simply this: to be allowed to set up a small school of Jewish learning in a remote part of Palestine. Seeing no harm in this modest request, Vespasian replied: "Sure. If I become Emperor, as you say, you may have your school."

Within a year, Ben Zakkai's prophecy was fulfilled, and Vespasian became Emperor of Rome. Shortly after, a Jewish academy was built in the town of Jabneh, north of Jerusalem. It was the very first yeshiva.

Where the synagogue and Torah were the foundations of Jewish worship, the yeshiva became the home of Jewish study. It was a school of law, where Jews would study the Torah and Talmud, and train to become rabbis.

In 70 C.E., the first Judean/Roman war came to an end. Jerusalem was invaded, and the Temple there, destroyed. But the yeshiva lived on!

Judaism and Christianity. What is the historical relation between the two faiths? How did one emerge from the other? These are complex questions. Let's backtrack a little.

During the last two centuries B.C.E., Judaism experienced a growth in popularity among peoples of the Hellenic world. For whatever conflicts there were between Greek authorities and the Hasidean Jews of Palestine, many Greeks took great interest in the books of the Torah, seeing them as an enlightened alternative to pagan worship practices of the day. How did this interest come about?

We recall that Jewish scholars in Babylonian exile a few centuries earlier had translated the Pentateuch into Aramaic, allowing Jews who could not read Hebrew to understand the scriptures. But Aramaic was not the only language of exile. Many Jews came to live in Greek-ruled Alexandria, in Egypt. For them, naturally, Greek had become their native tongue. And so, just as in Babylonia and Persia, Jews of this region felt the need for a translation too.

In a gesture of friendship to the Jews living under his rule, King Philadelphus of Alexandria initiated a great project. Seventy Jewish scholars were selected to translate the Torah into Greek. The Septuagint, as it was called, was completed around 250 B.C.E., and it was to have a profound effect throughout the region for centuries to come.

It was not just for the Jews that the Septuagint was written. Philadelphus wanted a copy too! He recognized the great philosophy and wisdom contained in this collection of writings, and wanted to share it with others.

In time, the Septuagint became a "best seller" throughout Greece, and over the next couple of centuries, many Greeks, and even Romans, converted. By the first century C.E., over ten percent of the entire Roman population practiced Judaism in one form or another. A full third of this Jewish population were Greek and Roman converts.

Why the attraction? What was it about Judaism that appealed to so many?

For thousands of years, religion had followed a certain, predictable course. People looked up at the heavens and saw there a multitude of gods, each in charge of administering justice through natural disaster. Droughts, floods, disease, locust plagues, volcanoes and earthquakes were all seen as divine punishment from above.

Helpless before these tirades, people sought to ease the temper of their gods by making ritual sacrifices to them. But the gods were fickle, and people had little sense of being able to control their own fate in such a chaotic world. Such was the outlook for so many, for so long.

With the advent of Mosaic Law, and the writings of the Jewish Prophets, there emerged in the last millennium B.C.E., a new way of looking at things. Rather than many gods, the Jews observed one. And, in place of helplessness, they saw where they could make things better through their own actions. How one behaved became more important than how many goats one could bring to Temple for sacrifice. These were new and revolutionary ideas. The Septuagint helped popularize these ideas, and contributed greatly to the growing conversion rate during the Greek and Roman periods.

The greatest portion of Jewish converts came by way of the Essene sect. We recall from an earlier chapter how Judaism had divided into three distinct groups: the Sadducees, Pharisees, and Essenes. Many practices associated today with Christianity,

the rite of baptism for instance, started among the Essenes. As well, it was Essene practice to actively recruit new congregants by venturing out and preaching among the unconverted.

Early into the Common Era (the period during and after Christ), growing familiarity with the ideas of Judaism, and the spread of the Essene movement, together, paved the way for Christianity.

Christ, we recall, was an Essene Jew. His period of active involvement as a preacher lasted for about three years, roughly between 30 and 33 C.E. Following his death, Christ's followers continued his ministry, attracting ever more numbers.

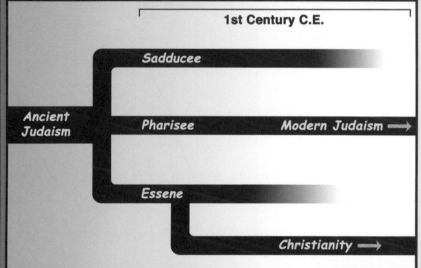

For a time, Christianity remained a sect of Judaism. That is, to become a Christian, one first converted to Judaism, and then entered the Christian fold. To make the religion more attractive to outsiders, certain requirements, such as the strict dietary laws, were dropped. Gradually, Christianity came to resemble something other than Judaism altogether. By 50 C.E., it had evolved into a new religion in its own right.

The destruction of the Temple in Jerusalem in 70 C.E. marked the end of the Sadducees. The rise of Christianity brought the Essene movement to a close. It was left to the Pharisees to carry Judaism forward into the future.

Judaica Crossword Puzzle 2

Down

1. The Greek Torah. (Chapter 12)
2. He instructed people to "walk humbly with thy God." (Chapter 6)
3. The Commandments were carried in this. (Chapter 5)
4. This nation conquered Persia in 334 B.C.E. (Chapter 9)
5. This Persian king allowed Jews to return to Judah. (Chapter 7)
6. This branch of Judaism gave rise to Christianity. (Chapter 12)
7. "For I desire righteousness, not sacrifice" were his words. (Chapter 6)
8. The language of exile in Persia. (Chapter 7)
9. The first book of the Torah to be written. (Chapter 6)
10. A Greek term meaning "scattering." (Chapter 11)
11. Rabbi _____ Zakkai. (Chapter 11)
12. He led the Greeks to victory. (Chapter 9)

Across

1. He became king of Judah in 638 B.C.E. (Chapter 6)
2. Five books put together in 444 B.C.E. (Chapter 7)
3. During Hanukkah, we celebrate the _____ revolt. (Chapter 9)
4. The Greek word for "assembly". (Chapter 7)
5. They warned of dangers. (Chapters 5 and 6)
6. Ben Zakkai traveled in a coffin to meet with this Roman general. (Chapter 11)
7. He presented the Pentateuch in Judah. (Chapter 7)
8. This nation conquered Judah in 586 B.C.E. (Chapter 6)
9. He said…"Everyone worshippeth the work of his own hands." (Chapter 6)
10. This nation conquered Babylonia in 539 B.C.E. (Chapter 6)
11. Short form for "Before Common Era."

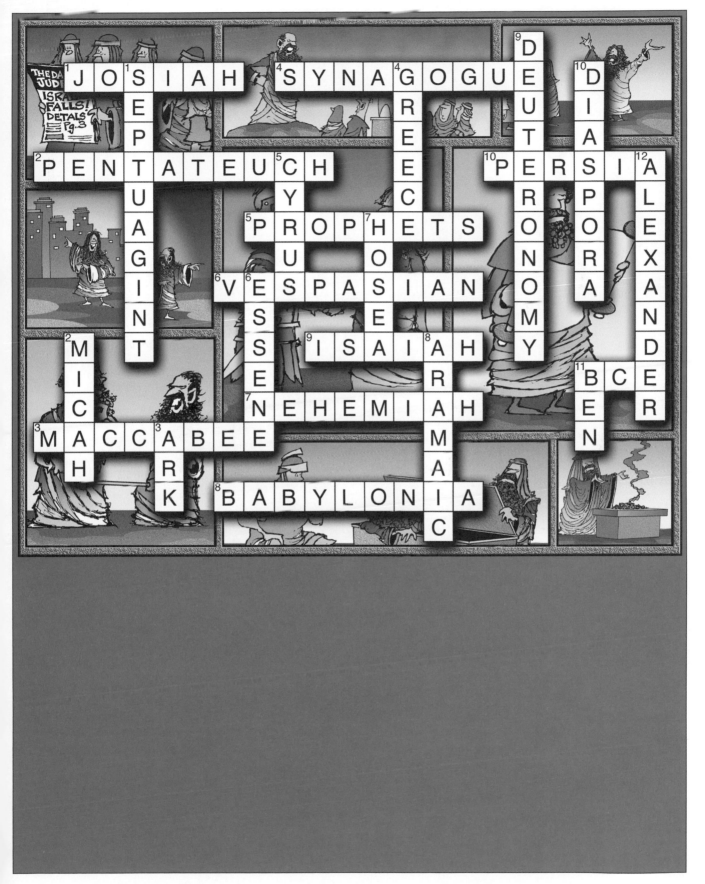

45

In its first three hundred years, Christianity evolved as a religion, a spiritual movement, and a political organization. It grew in numbers, and eventually, in influence. But over this time, it was also illegal. Having been outlawed by the Roman authorities in the first century C.E., Christians practiced their faith at great peril. When caught and tried, they were often thrown into lion dens for the amusement of Colosseum-goers.

It was not uncommon for Christians on the run from Roman authority to find refuge in Jewish homes. For whatever differences there now were between the two faiths, they did share common traditions. And Jews could recognize in the Christians a reflection of their own struggles over the centuries to survive in hostile lands.

We as Jews can understand the sting of persecution. It has been a sad reality throughout much of our history. But it is important, also, to make distinctions. Certainly, at various times, Jews and Romans did not get along. Following each war with Judea, Rome exacted harsh punishments, such as when Hadrian banished all Jews from Palestine. But was this religious persecution? Was this anti-Semitism?

To the Romans, the Jews were a recognized people. They had a kingdom, and an accomplished history, which the Romans knew, full well, predated their own. Conflicts between Jews and Romans were, by and large, of a nationalistic nature. They concerned land, statehood, and

power. Hatred toward Jews as individuals, or toward Judaism as a religion, was rare. There was a general respect the Romans had for Jewish philosophy and traditions. Jews were granted full citizenship, and filled high office in Roman business, law, and government.

Christians, on the other hand, were seen as a cult. They kept mostly to themselves. They were outsiders, viewed by many with scorn.

Religious persecution we might define as the hostile targeting of a distinct group of people based on their faith. This certainly would describe the Christian experience in the first three centuries C.E. Whenever Romans looked for scapegoats, the Christians were always a handy target.

It is an interesting observation to make at this point, because we will see how, just a few centuries ahead, the roles of Jews and Christians became switched.

In spite of persecutions, the Christian movement grew. By the early fourth century, over twenty percent of Rome's population was Christian. It had become the single largest religious organization in the empire, as Judaism had been three centuries earlier. As the Christian population grew, political winds began to shift as well. Roman rulers came to see disadvantages in alienating such a large portion of the population. General acceptance, in time, led to full-scale embrace. In the year 324, Emperor Constantine, a recent convert, declared Rome a "Christian nation." In the three centuries since its beginnings in Galilee, Christianity rose from a fledgling sect and reviled minority, to becoming the official faith of the Roman Empire.

Following Constantine, Jews suddenly found themselves no longer in the Roman world as they knew it. They were now in a Christian world. And life did change.

We sometimes use the term "paradigm shift" to mean one, all-encompassing instance of change. The birth of Christian Rome was such a shift. Up until this point, Jews and Christians did not concern themselves much with one another. That the Christians proclaimed Christ their messiah while the Jews did not was of limited importance. Certainly, the Romans had no interest in the matter. But as Christianity entered the realm of Roman politics in the fourth and fifth centuries, new attitudes toward Jews started to emerge. Central to the Christian doctrine was that it was a universal faith: all were to be converted. A couple centuries earlier, the Christians had given up trying to convert the Jews, focusing instead on pagans. Should they now demand that all Jews become Christian too?

By the dawn of the fifth century, the Jews stood as the single largest unconverted mass in Rome. To the new Christian Roman rulers, their presence alone was a challenge to Christian doctrine and authority. It is in this growing shadow between Judaism and Christian Rome, in the last phase of the empire, that we see the first inklings of modern anti-Semitism. It is a subject we will return to as we venture into the middle ages and beyond. For now, let's take one last look at Rome…

You have, no doubt, heard about the "fall of Rome." When and how did it "fall" exactly? Did it happen in an afternoon? Or, was it more a gradual period of decline?

By the time of Constantine's conversion, Rome had become too big for its own good. Cracks started to form in its foundation. In 395, Rome divided into two separate empires: the western empire, with its capital in Rome, and the eastern, or Byzantine empire, whose capital was established in Constantinople. Just as with Israel and Judah almost a thousand years earlier, the Roman kingdoms bickered and competed with one another. They were ripe for invasion.

On the outskirts of both empires at this time, lurked a host of emerging "barbarian" societies. Goths and Vandals in the north, and Mongols, or "Huns", from the east, each eyed the Roman domains with envy. Over the course of the fifth century, the empires experienced wave after wave of attack from these invading forces. With their armies depleted, and economy in ruin,

Rome was slowly pecked away, until it was no more.

In 475, a fourteen-year-old boy named Romulus Augustulus was crowned emperor of western Rome. Less than a year later, in 476, he was forcibly removed by the conquering Goths. While few knew it at the time, the Roman Empire had ended. The middle ages had begun.

What do we mean when we say "the Middle Ages"? How does one age just end, and another begin?

We recall from the last chapter that the Roman Empire came to its end, more or less, in the late fifth century. Barbarian armies from the north and east took turns "sacking" different parts of the western empire, breaking it into smaller regions. Each broken-off "chunk" came under the rule of foreign conquerors, creating new independent nations in the process.

Goths from Germany took over Spain and Italy. Vandals became rulers of France and some sections of North Africa. To the east and south sprawled the Byzantine world; the last remaining portion of what had once been the Roman Empire.

The world was now, quite suddenly, in a very different shape. What had been one single mighty empire, under the rule of one leader, was now a whole mish-mash of smaller countries; the bits and pieces that would become the nations of Europe.

The next ten centuries or so of this newly shaped world is the period we know as "the Middle Ages." It is a period we will examine for several chapters. The stories of many nations, several religions, and at least three continents we will see intertwine. And, we will come to know something of the experience of Jews, and role of Judaism, in the nations of this period.

14th Century German Illuminated Haggadah for Passover

Let's begin our journey through the Middle Ages by posing a question. It is one we have asked before. How did the Jews survive? What held them together as a people during this time? What kept their faith intact while their lives were spread so far and wide?

Fifteen hundred years earlier, the Jews themselves had a mighty kingdom. Gradually, over a thousand years, they lost hold of it. They became scattered among many nations. The Diaspora, which had begun in Babylonia and Persia, was made complete by Hadrian during the Roman period. By the time of the Middle Ages, the Jews had been, for a thousand years already, a "wandering people."

In the course of their wanderings, the Jews learned to adapt. Where Temple practices were not easily portable, the Torah was. And, where the laws of the Torah could not meet the needs of changing times, the Talmud took precedent.

A few chapters ago, we read the story of Rabbi Jochanan Ben Zakkai, and his journey in a coffin to visit general Vespasian. His great accomplishment, we recall, was the building of the first yeshiva, a university dedicated to the study of the Talmud. It was this book, and this institution of learning which, together, helped preserve Judaism throughout the Middle Ages. For this reason, we might also call this period the "Talmudic Age."

Consider, for a moment, a very modern problem; whether one should, or should not, drive a car on the Sabbath. Early in the twentieth century, a yeshiva court ruled that driving an automobile is a form of labor. The Torah, as we know, forbids us to work on the Sabbath. And so, driving to Shul was prohibited. This law was

fine when neighborhoods were closely knit, and the synagogue was in walking distance for all. But, in time, cities expanded, and suburbs appeared. Communities became spread apart. Many Jews no longer lived in the same area of town as their Shul. Should they still be expected to walk?

It was questions of this nature which rabbis of the Talmudic age examined, and argued over. Practical solutions to new and unfamiliar problems were arrived at through their collective debates. Where the Torah provided the basic laws of Mosaic justice, the Talmud helped Jews in different lands interpret these laws, and make sense of them. Remember, by the time of the Middle Ages, the Torah was about one thousand years old. Life had changed much in that time.

Throughout Europe and the Byzantine east, Talmudic education flourished. Yeshivas sprouted up everywhere. By the time of the Renaissance, some centuries later, Talmudic traditions of the Middle Ages had led to new areas of thought entirely, beyond the realm of religion. Scholars looked to the future. They studied science, and sought rational explanations for the mysteries of the world around them. They became philosophers, poets, and writers of fiction.

Portrait of Baruch Spinoza, unknown artist, 1665

The yeshiva schools produced great thinkers, some of whom came to influence western culture. Moses Ben Maimon, or "Maimonides", was a Spanish-born Jew of the twelfth century. He wrote great works in the areas of religion and philosophy, and helped restore popular interest in the writings of the Prophets. Baruch Spinoza, from the Netherlands, lived a few centuries later. He, too, would have an enormous impact on western thought.

A thousand years earlier, the Jews had lived among the Greeks. From their contact with this culture, Jewish scholars developed an appreciation for science and rational thinking. This interest was reborn in the yeshivas of Europe and the Byzantine during the Middle Ages. Greek traditions of science, brought to Christian Europe by Diaspora Jews, reintroduced the world to rational thought, and paved the way for the Renaissance.

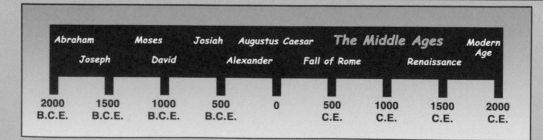

| Abraham | Moses | Josiah | Augustus Caesar | | The Middle Ages | | Modern Age |
| Joseph | David | | Alexander | | Fall of Rome | Renaissance | |

| 2000 B.C.E. | 1500 B.C.E. | 1000 B.C.E. | 500 B.C.E. | 0 | 500 C.E. | 1000 C.E. | 1500 C.E. | 2000 C.E. |

Very early into the middle ages, the new barbarian kings of Europe were converted to Christianity. The nations that formed under their rule, Italy, France, Spain, and Germany, were governed as Christian states.

Scattered among these states were isolated Jewish populations. Some had settled in Germany as early as the third century, and many in Italy had been there since before the time of Christ.

By the end of the tenth century, the Christian domain stretched as far as Poland, Scandinavia, and Russia. Over the course of the middle ages, Jews increasingly found themselves a vulnerable minority in an ever-expanding majority. How did Jews of this time fit in among their Christian neighbors? What was life like for Jews of medieval Europe?

The Christians of feudal Europe lived in a class system, which offered few options. People were divided into three general categories: the nobility (rulers and soldiers), the clergy (the church), and the peasantry (all the rest). Which group you wound up in was pretty much decided from birth. And most people, it seems, were born peasants.

55

Medieval Europe was a world of a few "haves", and many, many, many "have-nots." The toil of millions of peasants produced wealth that only a few nobles enjoyed.

What had not yet developed in the nations of Europe, early on, was a substantial mercantile, or "middle-class." That is, a portion of society that is not of the nobility or clergy, but is *not* poor either. Craftsmen, manufacturers, merchants, traders, and many others make up the mercantile class. For any nation to "get on its feet", it needs people with such skills. Industry and commerce grow with their efforts.

For some fifteen hundred years, the Jews had been a scattered people, inhabiting many lands. They engaged in trade with many peoples, and had learned much. They became skilled artisans and successful merchants. Compared to the peasants of Europe, the Jews were well traveled. And, through the growing yeshiva school system, many were highly educated.

Rulers of Europe saw, in the Jews, the very qualities of industry needed to build their young empires. To theses rulers, the Jews were a "ready-made" mercantile class.

At the beginning of the ninth century, Charles the Great, or "Charlemagne", became ruler of one enormous kingdom combining France and Germany. Quickly into his reign, he extended his hand in friendship to Jews far and wide. He allowed them many freedoms. Some even rose to positions of influence in Charlemagne's court.

The Jews were welcomed because they had skills that Charlemagne needed for his kingdom to grow. Other nations invited Jews for the same reasons. And over the middle ages, the Jewish populations of Europe played a significant role in the development of trade and industry.

While the political rulers of Europe welcomed the Jews, the Christian church had mixed feelings. When attempts were made to convert them, the Jews resisted. Should they be forced to become Christian?

Portrait of Pope Gregory the Great, by Francisco de Zurburan, 1627

Attitudes varied. Early in the middle ages, Pope Gregory the Great urged the church to accept the Jews, and not force them to convert. But, the church would not always be so generous. At different times and places, Jews were restricted in their freedoms. Fearful that Christians might become influenced by "Jewish thinking" church leaders looked for ways to keep Jews out of Christian society. Certain laws prohibited them from holding certain posts, entering some professions, and from socializing with their Christian neighbors.

And so, the Jews of Europe were welcomed, but they were also outsiders; sought for their skills and industry, but at times, scorned for their beliefs and traditions.

Jews were kept apart from the Christian world in many ways. But, at the same time, they were also free of the bonds of the European class system. They were allowed to engage in business, and many prospered.

Envy of the freedom and success achieved by the mercantile class took root in the "have-not" populations of Europe. Those chained to the bitter cycle of feudal peasantry came to resent those who were free of it. By the late middle ages, these resentments, mixed with suspicion over religious differences, led to widespread backlashes against the Jews, and others. A few lessons back, we first encountered the term *anti-Semitism*. In the Christian Crusades of the eleventh and thirteenth centuries, we see this tragic ingredient of our history truly emerge.

The middle ages are a period we usually associate with events in Europe. But, throughout the world at this time, the stories of many young empires were unfolding.

Across the Mediterranean, in the Arabian desert-regions, there emerged early in the seventh century a civilization founded on the new Islamic

faith introduced by the prophet Mohammed. Islam had much in common with Judaism. Inspired by Moses and the Jewish prophets, Mohammed and his followers believed in one invisible God. They condemned the worship of idols, and, like the Jews, placed great value on knowledge and education.

Islamic Kingdom
of the Middle Ages

By the eighth century, the Muslim Empire included much of the Byzantine down through North Africa, and, for the next seven hundred years or so, posed the largest single cultural, spiritual, and military challenge to Christian Europe.

Among the Muslims lived many Jews. We recall from previous chapters how Jews were already living in these regions as far back as the sixth century B.C.E. Many who were in exile, established communities, which, in time, fell under Byzantine, then Muslim rule. As well, following the first Judean/Roman war and the destruction of the second Temple in 70 C.E., quite a few more Jews resettled in the vast Arab domains beyond Palestine. The descendants of these Jews experienced the middle ages in a Muslim world.
It is a period and place often described as a Jewish "Golden Age."

As mentioned before, the Muslims revered education. They took seriously the study of science, and sought to expand their knowledge of the natural world. As well, they had great respect for others with similar interests.

Since the time of the Greek empire, the Jews, too, had developed a passion for science. Their knowledge in areas of mathematics, astronomy, and medicine was of much interest to the Muslims.

Over the course of the middle ages, the two cultures lived side by side, engaging in trade, and exchanging scientific knowledge. The Jews earned a nickname: "The people of the book." It was a term of respect and admiration given them by their Muslim hosts.

It is important to understand, as we view the tragic state of Jewish/Muslim relations in the world today, that for a lengthy period of history, the two peoples lived together in relative harmony.

Meanwhile, back in Europe...

By the eleventh century, the Christian church had become quite zealous. Those who still resisted conversion were deemed "infidels" and "heretics." In an effort to assert its supremacy, the church now looked to convert people by force. And, there emerged among some religious leaders an idea: to embark on a mission to "free" the Holy Land from its Muslim, or "infidel" rulers, and claim Jerusalem for Christianity.

Entry of the Crusaders into Constantinople, by Gustave Dore, Nineteenth Century

Between the eleventh and thirteenth centuries, a series of Christian crusades were launched. Mighty armies stormed across Europe and on to the Holy Land, leaving an awful trail of destruction in their wake. Because Jews resisted conversion to Christianity, they too were considered infidels. Many Jewish homes were attacked. Christians who attempted to help their Jewish neighbors were treated the same. In some instances, whole towns were set ablaze. Dark times had arrived.

To make matters worse, these armies were often undisciplined and unruly. By the later crusades (there were seven major crusades in all), they were, by and large, not made up of professional soldiers. Convicts were granted pardons, and serfs given freedom in exchange for taking up arms. The crusades became, in the end, something of a violent looting party.

Late in the thirteenth century, the crusades finally came to an end. But difficult times did not. Early on in the middle ages, we recall, Jews had been welcomed, more or less, in the nations of Europe. But, by the eleventh century, the mood had changed. Jews found themselves increasingly isolated from the Christian world around them. In an effort to keep the two faiths separate, the church passed laws forcing Jews to live in assigned ghettoes. In 1215, Pope Innocent the Third took it a step further, requiring Jews to wear badges for religious identification.

Just as the Christians had been, back during the Roman period, Jews were now often made scapegoats. When the bubonic plague struck Europe in the mid-fourteenth century, rumors spread among the panicked peasantry that Jews somehow were responsible. Accused of poisoning the wells, and thus causing the epidemic, Jews became the targets of unruly, violent mobs seeking revenge.

Between the eleventh and sixteenth centuries, the Jews of Western Europe underwent a series of expulsions. England, France, Spain, Italy, and a few other nations posed ultimatums: convert to Christianity, or leave. Most Jews chose expulsion.

And so, the Jewish populations of Europe migrated eastward to Germany, Poland, Austria, Lithuania, and in time, far off Russia. Two thousand years had come and gone since the period of Babylonian exile, and the Jews found themselves, still, a wandering people.

In the previous chapter, we learned about the expulsion of Jews from Western Europe during the late middle ages. There were many expulsion stories in that time, all of them tragic and bitter. Let's take a close look at one of them…

In the late fifteenth century, Spain was home to the largest Jewish population in Western Europe. One out of every ten Spaniards at this time was a Jew. The Jews played a vital part in Spanish culture, trade, and economics, and had great influence on the nation.

As in many countries at the time, restrictive laws prevented Spanish Jews from entering certain professions and from participating fully in public life. But there was a way around these obstacles. A "magic key" was offered to the Jews of Spain:

conversion. If Jews accepted Christ as the messiah, and submitted to baptism, they would be welcomed fully in Spanish society. Doors would open for them that would otherwise stay shut.

In hopes of broadening their opportunities in life, many Jews chose to become "conversos," abandoning their religion entirely. For a time, conversion to Christianity had its desired effect. Conversos found they could move about in Spanish society freely.

But Spain of the fifteenth century was a place of growing unrest. As the Jewish and Muslim populations of Spain increased, so too did Catholic insecurities. Fearful of any influence that might weaken its hold on the nation, the church grew suspicious of outsiders. As well, religious revolt by Christian "heretics" threatened the institution from within. In an effort to root out heretical influence, the Catholic Church launched an investigation. It was called The Spanish Inquisition.

The Inquisition's main purpose was to restore the Catholic faith, and to expose the heresies of impious Christians (those whose faith was deemed "untrue" by the church). Following conviction, heretics were then tortured in a variety of unspeakable ways.

Because their conversion to Christianity had been so recent, the conversos were widely suspected. In the course of its investigations, the Inquisition hauled many conversos before its court, and found that some had actually continued to practice their Jewish faith in secret. "Marranos" they were called, meaning "swine." Perceived as being "Christian on the outside, but Jewish on the inside", the treatment they were subjected to was particularly harsh.

The tragedy, and irony, of the story of the Spanish conversos is this: Out of a longing to be accepted by the Christian world around them, many Jews willingly abandoned their faith. But, the further they attempted to fit in, the more they were treated with suspicion and contempt. Strangely, outwardly practicing Jews were by and large, left alone by the Inquisition. "Phony Christians", it seems, were the target.

Official Order of Expulsion, signed by King Ferdinand and Queen Isabella of Spain in 1492

As the fifteenth century drew to a close, religious tensions mounted. In 1492, Queen Isabella and King Ferdinand, under pressure from the Catholic Church, signed an official order, expelling all Jews and Muslims from Spain. In all, around one hundred thousand Jews were suddenly homeless. Many headed for Portugal. Others went to the Islamic east, now under rule of the Ottoman Empire. Most, in time, found their way to Eastern Europe and Russia.

Over the late middle ages, Jews underwent expulsion time and time again. Different nations at different times found reasons to be rid of their Jewish populations, only to invite them back a century or two later. Life was a "not-so-merry go round."

During this period, we see the emergence of two institutions of European Jewish life: the ghetto, and the shtetl. We recall from a previous chapter how ghettos were already in use as early as the thirteenth century. Following expulsion from Spain, they became fixtures of cities across Europe.

The Jewish ghetto

The ghetto was a gated community, locked up at night from both outside and in. Its purpose was to socially isolate the local Jewish population, and limit its interactions with Christians to daytime business dealings. Ghettos were typically cramped and noisy. Because they were not allowed to own the land they lived on, Jews could not expand their ghetto walls. Instead, they built upward, creating, perhaps, the first ever high-rise apartment complexes.

Many European rulers claimed these ghettos were for the protection of their Jewish inhabitants. The protection they afforded was, in fact, little. But their isolating effect on the Jews of Europe would be enormous.

The Jewish shtetl

Further to the east, in Poland and Russia, Jewish life centered around the shtetl. These were small rural communities populated entirely by Jews. Here, Jewish interaction with the Christian world was limited, but not so scarce as in the ghettos of the west. The shtetls were not gated, allowing for more coming and going. They did, however, like the gated ghettos, serve to keep Jews separate.

This period of the ghetto and the shtetl, stretching right through to the nineteenth century, was a dark age for the Jews. Squeezed out of more and more professions, many were reduced to peddlers.

What do a people do when they can no longer see the horizon, when day-to-day existence is bleak, and life holds little hope? How might they find ways to maintain their faith, while trapped in a cage? Maybe they would use their imaginations, and seek worlds of the mind to take them far beyond the ghetto walls.

Out of the shtetls and ghettos of Europe during the late middle ages, new mystic strands of Judaism emerged. Like lamps dimly flickering in the dark, these new spiritual movements gave meaning, hope, and direction to Jewish life in difficult times. Two most prominent movements of the age were Kabbalah, and Hasidism.

Kabbalah was a strange mix of magic, numerology, and meditations on the mystical qualities of God. It was a cosmological quest; in part, an attempt to understand the universe. Hasidism, more a product of the eastern shtetls, was founded by Ba'al Shem Tov, in eighteenth century Poland. It sought to bring simple joy and rapture to daily Jewish life.

Talmudic traditions of learning had brought Jews to an age of reason and modern, rational thought. Kabbalah and Hasidism brought comfort in an age when things seemed to have little reason at all.

From what we have read so far of Europe in the late middle ages, we might imagine it to have been an era of utter darkness for the Jews. But this was not entirely so.

As the Spanish Empire crumbled over the sixteenth and seventeenth centuries, so too did Roman Catholic control of several regions of Europe. The Protestant Reformation, headed by Martin Luther in Germany, John Calvin in Switzerland, and John Knox in Scotland, led to the drawing of new religious and national boundaries. Out of this shuffle came new nations, with new religious attitudes. One such nation to arise at this time was Holland (the Netherlands).

Formed in the seventeenth century, the Dutch republic emerged as a beacon of hope and refuge to many. It was a place of great tolerance and diversity. At a time when Jews throughout much of Europe were forced to dwell in gated ghettos, The Jewish community of Amsterdam, Holland's great capital, moved about freely. They entered professions of their choosing, and were treated with respect and dignity.

The atmosphere of tolerance experienced by the Jews of seventeenth century Holland is well represented in the works of the great Dutch painter, Rembrandt Van Rijn. While not Jewish himself, Rembrandt had strong spiritual ties to Jewish culture and traditions. He chose to live and work in a Jewish section of town.

Many of his neighbors became good friends, and often appeared as subjects in his paintings. The humanity and warmth with which Rembrandt depicted his Jewish subjects says much about Holland at the time, and of the enlightened attitude of its citizens.

The Jewish Bride, by Rembrandt Van Rijn, 1669

Because of its great tolerance, and its central location in Europe, Holland was a meeting place of many cultures. And so it was that two main strands of Jewish tradition, Sephardic and Ashkenazi, crossed paths here.

Sephardic culture of Western Europe

Perhaps you have heard these terms before. What do they mean? What differences defined the Sephardim and Ashkenazim from one another? Quite simply, Sephardic Judaism was a product Western Europe (Spain, Portugal), whereas Ashkenazi culture came from the east (Germany, Poland, Russia). Religiously, there was little difference between the two. The distinction stemmed initially from language. The Sephardim of the west had maintained Hebrew and Aramaic in their worship, while a hybrid of Spanish and Hebrew called "Ladino" dominated much of day-to-day speech. Ashkenazi Jews from the east developed a language based on Hebrew and German, called "Yiddish."

In time, different languages came to parallel different cultures, with different songs, different sounding words and expressions. Both languages and cultures found expression in the life of seventeenth century Amsterdam.

Ashkenazi culture of Eastern Europe

Holland was to play another central role in Jewish history. In 1654, two-dozen Jewish/Dutch citizens set sail on a long journey across the Atlantic Ocean. Their final destination would be New Amsterdam (New York). They were the very first Jews we know of to settle in the "new world" of America. Many more would follow.

Holland of the seventeenth century was a nation in the midst of a "rebirth." Long-forgotten traditions of science and art were being rediscovered. The spirit of the Renaissance, which touched many nations, led to new ideas and new attitudes, and in the end, helped pull Europe right out of the middle ages.

Following the phase of European Enlightenment, over the eighteenth and nineteenth centuries, two other great developments would sweep the western world: the democratic and industrial revolutions.

In the late eighteenth century, on the other side of the Atlantic, the founders of the new "United States of America" made the following declaration:

"We hold these truths to be self-evident, that all men are created equal, that they are endowed by their Creator with certain unalienable Rights, that among these are Life, Liberty and the pursuit of Happiness."

Declaration of Independence, by John Trumbull, 1819

It was a bold statement for its time, or any. The Declaration of Independence gave hope to the idea that nations might one day be governed, not by kings, queens, or religious authorities, but by the people themselves.

Inspired by the success of the American Revolution, a democratic revolt was launched in France shortly after. The time of kings and queens seemed to be nearing its end. New modern states with democratic systems of government were starting to emerge.

For the Jews of Europe, these revolutions were liberating. As Napoleon's armies stormed across the continent, Jewish ghettos were unlocked and dismantled. In time, nations that had previously kept Jews out, such as England, welcomed them back.

The world that the Jews entered over the late eighteenth, and nineteenth century was one of rapid change. New technologies and industries were sprouting up all over. It was an increasingly secular world, where citizenship stood above religion, where constitutions ensured peoples' rights, and where it seemed the Jews might have a chance of fitting in.

Along with these great changes came new opportunities. Limitations imposed on the Jews throughout the middle ages were being slowly removed. Jewish citizens of America and western/central Europe found themselves engulfed in a new spirit of patriotism, one that overshadowed religious difference. In 1874, England elected its first (and only) Jewish Prime Minister, Benjamin Disraeli. A country that had banished all Jews from its borders, now accepted this descendant of Abraham as head of state.

Benjamin Disraeli, Great Britain's first Jewish Prime Minister

A new kind of Jewish identity was emerging: a modern, assimilated, equal member of society.

We recall from the previous chapter how Napoleon's exploits were a liberating force for the Jews of Europe in the late eighteenth, and early nineteenth century. While campaigning in Palestine in 1799, Napoleon made the following proclamation to the small, local Jewish population there:

"Rightful Heirs of Palestine!... The Great nation [France] which does not trade in men and countries as did those who sold your ancestors unto all peoples hereby calls on you not indeed to conquer your patrimony, nay, only to take over that which has been conquered and, with that nation's warranty and support, to maintain it against all comers...

Hasten! Now is the moment which may not return for thousands of years, to claim the restoration of your rights among the population of the universe which has been shamefully withheld from you for thousands of years..."

Napoleon was simply saying here that Jews should feel they have a right to call Palestine their home, and in doing so could expect the support of France. His attempts to rally enthusiasm for a Jewish homeland in Palestine did not meet with success. But it was an early hint at things to come. Just over a century later, in 1917, Lord Arthur James Balfour of Britain signed his name to the now historic "Balfour Declaration." It expressed official recognition by a leading power of the newly emerging modern state of Israel:

"His Majesty's Government view with favor the establishing in Palestine of a national home for the Jewish people, and will use their best endeavors to facilitate the achievement of this object."

Lord Arthur Balfour, Great Britain's Foreign Secretary, and author of the Balfour Declaration in 1917

In the century or so from the time of Napoleon's proclamation to the signing of the Balfour Declaration, there occurred a mighty awakening. A distant dream, still buried in the hearts of Jews the world over slowly stirred to consciousness. Ancient yearnings for a faraway place called Israel now found expression in a movement called Zionism.

What motivated Jews at this point in history to undertake such a journey? What prompted them to return once again to their ancestral and spiritual homeland of Israel? To begin with, we must understand that Jews had never completely left the Middle East. In scattered, small communities in Jerusalem, Safed, Jaffa, and Hebron, a Jewish element had always remained in Palestine.

But for Jews of the Diaspora, those scattered throughout Europe, America, and elsewhere, Palestine was at most, but a dream. How did this dream transform, over the late nineteenth century, into a reality?

In the mid-nineteenth century, the world's entire Jewish population was a little less than five million. Over seventy percent lived in Eastern Europe and Russia. The great periods of enlightenment and revolution, which had swept Western and Central Europe, somehow never really took root in the east. Russia remained a backward, impoverished region, in many ways still trapped in the middle ages. Isolated from the changes going on in the west, Russia was ruled by czars (kings), and the vast majority of its inhabitants were serfs (peasants).

Jews living in Russia at this time were confined to certain regions, and prohibited from traveling freely. They knew little of the freedoms and prosperity enjoyed by Jews of the more progressive, industrial, and increasingly democratic west. Ancient hatreds, going back through the middle ages, still lingered. Russian Christians were raised on folk tales that demonized and cast suspicion on the Jews.

Following the assassination of Czar Alexander the second in 1881, a wave of anti-Jewish violence erupted. Organized riots, or "pogroms", were set loose on Jewish communities to punish them for somehow being involved. Just as in the days of the plague, Jews found themselves

blamed for every imaginable catastrophe. Near the end of the nineteenth century, and into the twentieth, the pogroms only worsened, spreading through Poland and the Ukraine. Being Jewish in these regions at this time was truly a hazard.

As anxieties mounted, Jews began leaving Russia and Eastern Europe. They left in the millions, hoping for a better life elsewhere. The vast majority headed for the United States. A few, excited and inspired by dreams of a Jewish homeland, made the epic journey to Israel. By 1903, some twenty-five thousand Russian Jews had settled there.

In Western Europe, things were not as bleak. Having regained entry into nations that had once kept them out, Jews found a world of opportunity waiting for them. They became doctors, scientists, businessmen, politicians, and in one case as we have seen, a British Prime Minister.

And yet, for all the progress seen in the west, something ugly still lurked below the surface. Where religious intolerance was no longer in fashion, bigotry lived on in other forms. In the nineteenth century, even among the enlightened nations of Western Europe, there were always those who saw Jews as the "enemy."

In 1894, a French army captain named Alfred Dreyfus was put on trial for treason. Dreyfus, a Jew, had been accused of sharing military secrets with the Germans. Popular opinion was against Dreyfus, his Jewish background being used to arouse scorn. He was convicted and imprisoned. Years later, when the case was reopened, it was found that Dreyfus had in fact been framed by a zealous anti-Semitic fellow officer. Being Jewish, it turned out, had been Dreyfus' only "crime." He was pardoned and released. But the "Dreyfus Affair" cast a shadow, and left many Jews wondering: "Will we ever be truly accepted?"

Alfred Dreyfus

Among the many Jewish citizens of Europe, shocked and dismayed by the ugly sentiments exposed by the Dreyfus case, was a young journalist named Theodor Herzl. Born in Budapest, and raised in Vienna, Herzl struggled with issues of anti-Semitism, and became the leading voice of Zionism in the late nineteenth century. He organized the first Zionist Congress in 1897, and worked tirelessly to raise badly needed funds for the cause.

Theodor Herzl

And, upon touring Eastern Europe and Russia, inspired many Jews there, weary of poverty and fearful of pogroms, with his vision of a homeland in Palestine.

Herzl would not live to see his dream of Jewish nationhood realized in full. But the work he had begun was carried on by Chaim Weizmann, a renowned biochemist, whose influence on Lord Balfour helped bring about the great declaration in favor of a Jewish state. The modern state of Israel was not yet born. But its foundations had been laid.

Chaim Weizmann

The Touro Synagogue in Newport, Rhode Island

The oldest standing Jewish worship hall in the United States of America is the Touro Synagogue in Newport, Rhode Island. It has been home to the congregation Yeshuat Israel since 1763. In 1789, just ten years before Napoleon's great proclamation to the Jews of Palestine, President George Washington made a visit to the Newport congregation. There, he gave a statement, which included the following passage:

"May the children of the Stock of Abraham, who dwell in this land, continue to merit and enjoy the good will of the other inhabitants, while everyone shall sit in safety under his own vine and fig-tree, and there shall be none to make him afraid."

In the final portion of his statement, Washington quotes the great Jewish Prophet, Micah (4:4). It was a fitting touch on a most profound and eloquent moment. Washington's address to the Newport congregation established that Jews would be respected and welcomed in this new republic, and not just "tolerated." It set the tone for the Jewish experience in America.

Never before in the long age of Diaspora was there a nation in which Jews would play such a vital role from the beginning. We recall from a previous chapter how Dutch Jews were settling in New Amsterdam as early as the mid-seventeenth century. They were few in numbers, and of largely Spanish and Portuguese descent. These first Jews to settle in the new world brought with them Sephardic traditions from Western Europe, and established the first Jewish communities in America.

Over the next few hundred years, many more Jews would set sail for the new world. By the time of the American Revolution, some twenty-five hundred Jews in total inhabited the colonies. By 1880, their numbers had jumped to two hundred and thirty thousand.

As new waves of Jewish immigrants came pouring in, new languages and customs were introduced. Over the eighteenth and nineteenth centuries, many German Jews came to the shores of America, and very quickly outnumbered the original Spanish Jewish population. Jews from Germany settled far and wide. Many became

peddlers and small-time merchants, traveling salesmen roaming the American horizon. In time, their businesses grew, becoming thriving commercial successes. The first department stores in America ("Gimbel Brothers", "Macy's", and others) were the achievements of these early German Jewish migrants.

In the late nineteenth, and early twentieth century, we recall, dark times were sweeping across Eastern Europe and Russia. And so it was that the next (and largest) wave of Jewish migration to America came from these troubled regions. From the shtetls of Poland and Russia, they came by the millions in overcrowded cargo ships, seeking refuge, and hopes for a brighter future.

Welcoming these newcomers as they arrived in New York Harbor was a great monument given by France to the United States: The Statue of Liberty. Like a mythic presence it must have seemed to the millions it greeted. Affixed on the monument's mighty pedestal is an engraved plaque, bearing the following poem:

"Keep, ancient lands, your storied pomp!" cries she
With silent lips. "Give me your tired, your poor,
Your huddled masses yearning to breathe free,
The wretched refuse of your teeming shore.
Send these, the homeless, tempest-tossed to me.
I lift my lamp beside the golden door!"

*Portrait of Emma Lazarus,
by T. Johnson, 1872*

These words were written by the Jewish American poet, Emma Lazarus. Her eloquence spoke to the hopes of all immigrants, Jew and non-Jew alike, struggling to leave fear and poverty behind and to begin life anew.

The "huddled masses" of this period began their American journey in the vast immigration hall on Ellis Island, off the tip of Lower Manhattan, in New York City. It was a perplexing and unsettling place to find oneself after such a long, difficult voyage.

Ellis Island, in New York Harbor

Between the years 1892 and 1924, some twelve million bewildered immigrants shuffled through the gates of Ellis Island for inspection. Two million were Jews. Few could speak English. Most arrived penniless. Some

were turned back on grounds of ill health. Those granted entry found themselves suddenly with new names and new identities, facing an uncertain future in a land they knew little about.

After the Ellis Island ordeal, a host of destination points awaited the new Jews of America. They settled throughout the eastern seaboard, in Boston and Philadelphia. Some ventured to Pittsburg, and others still further west to Chicago and St. Louis. But a vast portion remained in New York City, in a section of town called the "Lower East Side."

By 1915, some three hundred and fifty thousand Jews were living on the Lower East Side. It is a place with enduring ties to the Jewish American experience. It was cramped, crowded, and an altogether miserable experience for many. Thankless jobs at garment industry "sweatshops" offered meager livings for some. Others peddled wares in the street. Quite a few begged.

The harshness of life on the Lower East Side was matched by the industry and creativity it inspired. Out of this cobbled maze of tenements came writers, physicians, judges, and poets, gangsters and scholars; all manner of driven humanity, good and bad alike. Some rose to great prominence, like Louis Brandeis, who in 1916 became the first Jewish Supreme Court judge.

Louis Brandeis, U.S. Supreme Court Judge from 1916 to 1939, photograph by Harris and Ewing, 1916

Of the many contributions made to American culture by New York's Lower East Side, perhaps the most enduring came from the field of entertainment. The Yiddish Theatre, brought over from Europe, continued to thrive in the largely Polish and Russian neighborhoods of Lower Manhattan. My own great, great grandfather was such a performer. A comedian and musician known as "Sonya the Bard", he played at weddings and parties.

"Sonya the Bard", an early twentieth century Yiddish Theatre performer in New York, and great/great grandfather to the author of this book

Louis B. Mayer, a central figure in the founding of the American film industry

From these traditional roots emerged new forms of entertainment. Standup comedy and the antics of vaudeville brought Jewish performers to new heights of celebrity. The Marx Brothers and The Three Stooges, both, were products of this time, place, and culture, taken to the age of film and television. It was two Lower East Side Jews, Samuel Goldwyn and Louis B. Mayer, who would venture to the California coast, and there build the foundations of the American film industry. From the Yiddish theatres of New York to the hills of Hollywood, a lively Jewish tradition found its way to the national, and in time international, stage.

Over the last several chapters, we have focused largely on the cultural experience of Jews in Europe and America. We have looked at political trends, economic and social conditions, and the emerging Jewish presence in the new world.

What about the Jewish religion? What course had Judaism taken over the bumps and turns of events? Were Jews in early twentieth century America practicing the same religion as their distant relatives across the Atlantic?

The ability to adapt to new surroundings has been a requirement of Jewish survival since ancient times. Babylonian Jews, we recall, discarded rituals of sacrifice and the institution of the priesthood in order to give the religion more portability.

So too, in the United States of the nineteenth and twentieth centuries, Jews found themselves, once again, in a strange land, struggling to sort out the nature of their faith.

In 1846, a rabbi from Czechoslovakia named Isaac Mayer Wise settled in Albany, New York, and there became leader of the Beth El congregation. Very quickly, he began making reforms. Choral singing was introduced. Men and women were permitted to sit together in the pews.

These were new and strange measures, perhaps too radical for many of the congregants who, in 1850, sent this rabbi on his way. Wise wound up heading to Cincinnati to become rabbi of the Bene Yeshurun congregation, where he remained for the rest of his life. At Bene Yeshurun, Isaac Wise established the principles and worship patterns of modern American (and Canadian) Reform Judaism.

Like the Jews of Babylonia and Persia, Greece and Rome, American Jews have become a largely assimilated population, dressing, eating, talking, and socializing in the fashion of their fellow citizens. Reform Judaism came about in recognition of this reality, allowing greater freedoms in certain areas of practice, such as dietary and ritual laws. As well, it has sought to be more inclusive. Women are today becoming Bat Mitzvah and ordained as rabbis; notably, Sally Jane Priesand who in 1972, became America's first female rabbi.

The exciting changes going on in American Judaism did not sit well with all. Coming largely from the Hasidic communities of Eastern Europe, late nineteenth and early twentieth century Jewish immigrants were surely startled by what they saw. The assimilated American Jew must have seemed of a different world to these newcomers. Shocked by the freedoms of the Reform community, many of the new Russian immigrants clung more tightly to their Orthodox traditions. But even among the Orthodox, changes became necessary to keep up with the times. An Modern Orthodox movement emerged, offering a "new-fashioned/old-fashioned" form of Judaism, one that preserved many aspects of Eastern European practice.

Spanning the gap between Orthodox and Reform, there emerged in America, in the early twentieth century, a compromise: Conservative Judaism, under the leadership of Solomon Schechter.

Rabbi Solomon Schechter, founder of the American Conservative Judaism movement, photograph circa 1895

Reform, Conservative, Reconstructionist and Orthodox together represent four faces of North American Judaism. They are four responses to the challenges of faith in the new world, three ways of grappling with the pull toward assimilation.

Beyond the realm of organized Judaism, there are many people of Jewish background living in North America who are completely assimilated, with no religious affiliations at all. They are Jewish only by virtue of parentage. America is, in many respects, the unofficial international home of the secular, assimilated Jew. In no other nation have Jews so widely blended in, leaving behind all traces of their religious heritage, nor risen to such heights of acceptance and success.

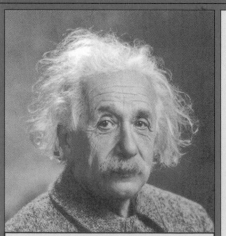

Albert Einstein, photograph by Oren Jack Turner, 1947

The very same words could be said of Jews living in Germany in the late nineteenth, and early twentieth century. Like Holland nearly three hundred years earlier, Germany had become a modern, progressive, and dynamic environment. Great leaps in the arts and sciences had boosted Germany's prestige. German composers, writers, physicists, and artists were being hailed worldwide. A new age of enlightenment had come, one that welcomed and included the Jews. Of the many Austro-German Jews whose names and works echo from this time, perhaps most stellar of all was a patent clerk from Vienna named Albert Einstein. His "Theory of Relativity" would alter the course of science and history.

But, like we saw in the case of Alfred Dreyfus in France, anti-Semitism was never far from the surface. By this time, religious intolerance was certainly no longer officially condoned by nations, keen to see themselves as modern and enlightened. But hatreds have a persistent way of adapting. New reasons to hate old enemies can always be found. Many Jews held tightly to the belief that they were, in fact, "German." But in the coming decades this illusion would be dashed.

The Jews of Germany and much of Europe would find themselves, in the first half of the twentieth century, caught in a nightmare the likes of which the world had never seen. Ancient hatreds would find expression in a most horrific form: The Holocaust.

The road that led from enlightenment to barbarism was a twisted one. World events, economic and political, played their part. Following its defeat in World War One, Germany limped into the 1920's, its economy in tatters, and its ego badly bruised. Scapegoats were sought to explain Germany's sorry condition. As had always been the case, Jews were a handy target. Claiming that Jewish influence had somehow "polluted" German resolve, many held the Jews accountable for the wartime defeat. Close to a hundred thousand Jews had, in fact, served in Germany's armed forces in World War I.

Some twelve thousand died. But arguments of this sort bore little weight with those hungry to lay blame.

Bitterness over the war, and desperation over economic fears, together produced a lethal mix. Germany had become a panicked nation. In 1933, the fears and hatreds that had been bubbling in Germany's depths churned their way to the surface in the form of Adolf Hitler. What follows is a saga more agonizing than any we have known.

No chapter in our history has been documented more thoroughly than the twelve years stretching between 1933 and 1945. It is the period that we, and the world, have come to know as the Holocaust. It haunts us still, posing many difficult, complex questions. How could it have happened? Might it have been stopped, or prevented altogether? Why did God not intervene? And, if God in fact did, why not sooner? Given the degree of horror, some are reduced to asking: *Is there even a God?*

The Holocaust emerged in stages, slowly tightening like a snake around its victim. Here is a basic chronology of events:

- In 1933, Adolf Hitler becomes Chancellor of Germany. The following year, he assumes complete command.
- Harassment of Jews begins immediately by gangs of Hitler's "Brown Shirts."
- In 1935, the Nuremberg Laws are passed, reducing Jews to non-citizens. They are forced out of all professions, and mixed marriages between Jews and non-Jews are prohibited. Within a year, seventy-five thousand Jews have left Germany, and eight thousand have taken their own lives in despair.
- In 1938, Germany annexes Austria. In November of that year, on a night now remembered as Kristallnacht ("Night of Broken Glass"), Jewish homes, synagogues, and businesses are burned and looted.
- In 1939, Germany invades Poland and Czechoslovakia, prompting World War Two. In that same year, large-scale deportations of German and Austrian Jews begin. As German forces storm across Europe, more and more Jewish populations fall into Hitler's grip.
- In 1940, Auschwitz is opened, and round-ups of Jews throughout occupied Europe are in full swing.
- In 1942 begins the implementation of "The Final Solution," Hitler's plan to eliminate Europe's entire Jewish population. Labor camps become designated death camps as, over the next three years, the true meaning of the word "holocaust" is realized.
- In 1945, Allied troops invade Germany, Hitler commits suicide, and the world awakes from a nightmare.

Entrance to Auschwitz-Birkenau concentration camp, Poland

Over the course of the Second World War, an estimated twelve million innocent people died at the hands of Nazi death squads. Some six million of them were Jews. Three million came from Poland alone. Their numbers are unfathomable. And the hideous journey it was for each and every one of them, unthinkable.

The images we have of the Holocaust are painful and upsetting. They invoke rage, and tears. They will not be the subject here. The agonies of millions are perhaps best pondered in silence and prayer. This chapter, instead, will concern the subject of courage, in two forms: the courage of Jewish resistance fighters, and the courage of compassionate Germans.

Considering the might and brutality of the Nazis, it is difficult to imagine what could have been done to combat them. It must be understood, though, that Jews did not resign to circumstances willingly. Many resisted, fighting the Germans on several fronts. Some joined up with non-Jewish partisan resistance groups. Others formed units on their own. It is estimated that around a hundred Jewish resistance groups were in operation throughout the war.

Most notable of all perhaps were the heroic combatants of the Warsaw ghetto in Poland. In 1940, a portion of Warsaw was converted by the Germans into a locked ghetto; a prison, in effect. Its purpose was to contain the Jews in preparation for

deportation to concentration camps. Five hundred thousand Jews in all were crammed into this section of the city. Life there was a desperate day-to-day struggle. Starvation and disease were rampant, claiming six thousand lives each month.

In the summer of 1942, three hundred thousand Jews were deported from the ghetto to Treblinka death camp. As word trickled back to the remaining Warsaw captives of the horrors at Treblinka, desperation gave way to rebellion. It seemed to many, at this point, there was nothing left to do but fight.

In early 1943, as the Nazis prepared for more deportations, a courageous band of Jews organized for battle. Led by twenty-three year-old Mordecai Anielewicz, a resistance army formed. With makeshift bombs and stolen weapons, they waged a dedicated war on German troops. For a month, the Germans were held back. Anielewicz led his brigade strategically, attacking from all angles. Like the Romans of two thousand years earlier, battling the besieged Judeans, the Germans had not expected such a revolt.

The Warsaw uprising came to its sad, inevitable end. As with the Romans, the Germans simply had more troops. But the efforts of Anielewicz and his followers must never be forgotten. They inspired others. In the summer of 1943, shortly after the uprising in Warsaw, prisoners rebelled at Treblinka. They seized weapons from the armory and set fire to the camp. Over three hundred escaped.

As we mourn for the millions who died in this dreaded time, let us also take heart in the courage of those who fought back.

Perhaps you have seen the film, "Schindler's List." It tells the true story of Oscar Schindler, a wealthy German businessman who saved the lives of over a thousand Jews during World War Two. Schindler entered the war as an industrialist, an opportunist looking to profit from wartime contracts with the German government. In the course of his dealings, he wound up with a sizeable labor force of Jewish slaves. As he came to know the people who worked under him, Schindler learned to see them, not as slaves, but as human beings; mothers, fathers, daughters and sons. He began to realize the horrors that were being inflicted, and which threatened the very lives of these people.

Something deep inside Oscar Schindler was moved. He resolved that, while he could not help those beyond his reach, "his Jews" would not suffer. Schindler had resources and connections. He bribed Nazi officers, forged documents, and spent millions, all to ensure the safety of his Jewish workers. He could have retired early from the war a wealthy man, but out of compassion, he chose to stay. As a result, twelve hundred lived.

What prompted Schindler to go to such lengths? We will likely never know. Perhaps, growing up next door to a rabbi, whose sons were Schindler's childhood best friends, played a part. Whatever the case, he acted with courage and grace.

Like Schindler, there were other decent, courageous Germans during the war who were moved to action. In Bernt Engelmann's book, "In Hitler's Germany," he gives accounts of ordinary German citizens, driven to extraordinary acts of courage and compassion. Among them was an elderly bakery shop owner in Berlin named Annie Ney. She was friendly and cheerful to all, even the Nazi officers who frequented her store for coffee and pastries.

What the Nazis did not know, though, was that Ney was part of a committed underground organization whose mission it was to smuggle as many Jews as possible out of Germany and to faraway safety. She worked with others, including a tailor, Herr Desch, whose business

trips to England before the war gave him opportunity to smuggle out Jewish children. They did not have the wealth or resources of Oscar Schindler. What they did have, though, was common decency, a respect for their fellow humans, and a great deal of courage.

Again, we might ask the question: why did they do it? What drove them to take such risks for the lives of complete strangers? In the following excerpt from Engelmann's book, he offers a first-hand account by a Jewish woman, Margarette Nussbaum, and her life-saving encounter with Annie Ney:

"frau Ney came over and shook hands with me. 'Everything is taken care of, Fraulein Nussbaum,' she said quietly. 'Our delivery man will be in Krefeld toward three this afternoon—we have a lot of bakery orders to drop off there. He'll pick you up at the Ostwald and take you to the house of good friends . . . and by Saturday at the latest you'll be in complete safety . . .' I didn't know what to say—I was trying to thank her and at the same time ask her why she was doing all this for a complete stranger. And she said—and I shall never forget this "Because I don't want to be ashamed of myself when I come to stand before my God." *

* (From "In Hitler's Germany", by Bernt Engelmann, published in the U.S. by Pantheon, 1986)

May God grant us all the courage and conviction of Annie Ney and others who acted selflessly in the name of humanity.

History will, on occasion, produce a miracle.

On May 14, 1948, the flag of the new state of Israel was raised for the first time, with full recognition by the nations of the U.N. Only three years earlier, World War Two had ended, and with it, the darkest chapter in Jewish, and certainly world, history. Out of the devastation of the

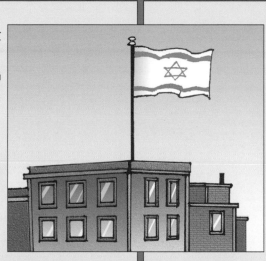

Holocaust came a stunning rebirth. Three thousand years after the Kingdom of David, and nineteen hundred years after the destruction of the second Temple, a new Jewish state was born in Palestine. Following a century of struggle, the Zionist dream was realized. Israel had become a nation.

It was by no means an easy feat. The road to sovereignty for the Jews of Palestine was a rocky one, with many pitfalls along the way.

We recall from a previous chapter how the efforts of Theodore Herzl, Chaim Weizmann, and others had set the stage in the late nineteenth and early twentieth century. Official recognition for the emerging Jewish state was then affirmed by Britain in the Balfour Declaration during World War One.

The following two decades saw the rapid growth of the Jewish population in Palestine. Between 1918 and 1936, one hundred and fifty thousand Jews settled there. Towns sprang up out of nowhere. A barren desert was transformed into fertile farmland. Schools, universities, and diverse industries blossomed. All the makings of a modern independent state were in place.

But there were complications. Before the arrival of Jewish settlers, Palestine had not been barren of inhabitants. Local Arab populations, living there for millennia, also called it home.

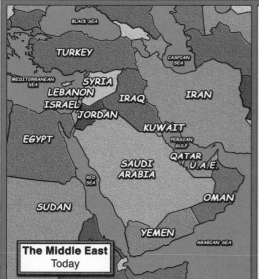

The Middle East
Today

Prior to the First World War, the region now commonly called the Middle East had belonged to the Turkish Ottoman Empire. Following the war, England and France took over, dividing up the region into the nations of Syria, Lebanon, Jordan, Iraq, and Saudi Arabia. It was a humiliating blow to the Muslim world. Between the intrusions of European powers and the increasing Jewish presence in Palestine, Muslim resistance grew. During the 1920's and 30's, clashes broke out, pitting Arab against Jew over land to which both groups claimed historical rights.

Making matters ever more urgent was the rise of Nazi Germany in the 1930's, which drove many to seek refuge in Palestine. By 1936, some sixty thousand German Jews had arrived in the Promised Land. And, with each new wave of Jewish settlers, Arab hostilities worsened.

Vladimir (Ze'ev) Jabotinsky, founder of the Jewish Defense Organization, or Haganah, in 1920

In light of this growing conflict, the Jews of Palestine realized they needed an army. Early Jewish pioneers formed a defense league, called the Hashomer. In time, this fledgling security force became the Haganah. Under the leadership of Russian-born Vladimir Jabotinsky, it formed the basis of what would become the Israeli army.

In 1936 the Haganah fielded 10,000 mobilized men along with 40,000 reservists. During the 1936-1939 Arab revolt in Palestine, it participated actively to protect British interests and to quell Arab rebellions.

Britain was certainly an ally of the Jews during World War Two, and it had demonstrated its support for the Jewish state twenty years earlier. But Palestine posed a great many problems for the British government. Britain's official position of support for Israel clashed with the reality of growing Arab discontent.

After the 1936 flare-up, in an effort to quell further hostilities, Britain opted to limit Jewish settlement in Palestine. It was an attempt to avert a Jewish/Arab war, but these restrictions served only to strengthen Jewish resolve for independence. By 1947, Britain had grown weary of its responsibilities in the Middle East. Jewish revolts in response to settlement restrictions, and the looming threat of an all-out war between the Arabs and Jews gave Britain good reason to leave. They handed the matter of Palestine over to the United Nations who, in November of that year, passed a resolution in favor of the Jewish state.

On May 14, 1948, as the last of the British forces departed, Jews in Palestine and throughout the world celebrated Israel's independence. The following day, Egypt, Jordan, Iraq, Syria, and Lebanon began their assault on the new nation.

What had been achieved on paper, now had to be secured on the battlefield. The Jews were greatly outnumbered. Their prospects did not look good. Three rounds of fighting took place over 1948 and '49. And, through it all, the Jews of Palestine held firm. They fought offensively, pushing far into enemy territory, and ultimately subduing the Egyptian forces, bringing the war to an end.

What the world saw, it had not expected. But, David slew Goliath just the same!

In 1949, Israel elected its first prime minister, David Ben-Gurion. At the time, six hundred and fifty thousand Jews lived in the new state. Over the next two decades, a million more would arrive. Israel bustled, and grew. Cities expanded. Agriculture and industry flourished, and a lively, dynamic society bloomed.

But Israel would always have to stand guard. For its first twenty-five years of existence, Israel faced continual threats from Egypt, who remained committed to destroying the Jewish state. In 1956, war broke out between the two nations, and then again in 1967; and again in '73. Each time, Egypt was beaten back, and Israel expanded its territories. Finally, in March of 1979, in the presence of U.S. president, Jimmy Carter, Menachem Begin, Israel's prime minister, and Egyptian president, Anwar Sadat, signed the now historic Camp David Peace Accords. Egypt became the first state in the region to officially and publicly recognize Israel's right to exist.

Left to Right, Egyptian president, Anwar Sadat, U.S. president, Jimmy Carter, and Israeli prime minister, Menachem Begin at Camp David in 1978

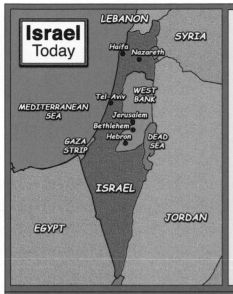

Israel Today

LEBANON
SYRIA
Haifa Nazareth
WEST BANK
Tel-Aviv
MEDITERRANEAN SEA
Jerusalem
Bethlehem
GAZA STRIP
Hebron
DEAD SEA
ISRAEL
EGYPT
JORDAN

Israel's struggle to assure its security continues to this day. The Arab populations fight also for a land they rightfully see as theirs. We pray that, one day, the spirit of conciliation will prevail, and peace will reign in the Middle East.

The miracle that is Israel stands today, in defiance of all odds. It is a legacy of faith, stretching back over centuries and millennia. That Jews should seek and succeed to rebuild their ancestral homeland after so long and painful an exile perhaps was inevitable. In the words of Golda Meir, prime minister of Israel from 1969 to 1974:

Golda Meir, prime minister of Israel from 1969 to 1974

"We have always said that in our war with the Arabs we had a secret weapon-no alternative."

A long time ago, in the land of Canaan, lived Jacob (Israel). He had twelve sons: Reuben, Simeon, Levi, Judah, Zebulun, Issachar, Dan, Gad, Asher, Nephtali, Joseph, and Benjamin. In the time of David, the distant

descendants of the sons of Jacob made up the Twelve Tribes of Israel. Of the eleven tribes who held territory, ten lived in the northern kingdom of Israel, or "Samaria." Only the tribe of Judah lived in the south.

The Assyrian invasion of 722 B.C.E. scattered the Israelites east of the Euphrates River and, it would seem, right off the

pages of history. Only Judah remained. It is from the single tribe of Judah that the words "Judaism", "Jewish", and "Jew" derive.

Where did the ten "lost tribes" go? Did they vanish utterly? Evidence suggests not entirely. It seems that some

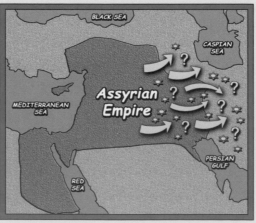

Israelite bands may have stayed partially intact in exile, and appear to have ventured well beyond Assyria.

Heading east into Asia are many peoples exhibiting peculiarities that hint at Hebrew origin. The "Yusuf" tribes of Afghanistan, for instance, claim to be the "Children of Joseph." They wear "Tzitzit" on their prayer shawls, and many adorn their hair with side locks curiously similar to the "Peyot" associated with Hasidic tradition. The "Pathans" of Pakistan, as well, share some customs with Judaism, including a kosher diet. Many have names like Gad, Asher, Samuel, and Israel. It is widely believed that they, too, represent a branch of the ten lost tribes.

And, the children of Israel may have ventured further still...

Jewish Phylactery (Tefillin)

There is a stirring idea, proposed by both Japanese and Jewish scholars, that the traditional Shinto religion of Japan has its roots in ancient Judaism. There are many similarities between the two religions. Like the *Phylactery* worn by orthodox Jews, Shinto priests wear the *Tokin,* a small black circular box worn on the forehead during prayer. Both have Tallit, or "Tzitzit" on their prayer garments.

Shinto Tokin

Shofar

The ceremonial blowing of a seashell horn by Shinto priests is strikingly similar to the sounding of the Shofar (rams horn) during Yom Kippur. As well, a portable Shinto shrine called the Mikoshi, by appearance, seems oddly reminiscent of the Ark of the ancient Israelites.

Shinto conch shell trumpet

And, there are parallels in language too. Scholars have found no less than five hundred words in both Japanese and Hebrew that share similar meaning and sound. The Hebrew word "Daber", meaning "to speak", and the Japanese word "Daberu", meaning "chatter", are but one example.

Is it possible that ancient Israelites escaping Assyrian captivity traveled as far eastward as Japan? Such a journey would likely have spanned generations, and involved numerous cultural interactions. We will probably never know the answer to this question. But the evidence is tantalizing.

Ark of the Israelites

Shinto Mikoshi

Whatever the case, it does seem clear that the Israelites of the eighth century B.C.E. did not disappear completely. In bits and pieces, scattered throughout Asia, Africa, and elsewhere, intriguing echoes of their presence remain.

Thoughts of this sort bring us closer to the question posed in the very first chapter of this book: who are the Jews?

Are we a race? At various times and places throughout history, we have been viewed as one. Spanish "conversos" were still considered to be "Jewish" by the courts of the Inquisition, in spite of their religious persuasion. Five centuries later, in Nazi Germany, similar ideas prevailed.

In its first two thousand years, Judaism came to include peoples from North Africa to southern Europe. The Israelites who Moses led out of Egypt were quite probably a broad mix, descendants of the sons of Jacob, surely, but many were enslaved in Egypt alongside the Hebrews for those four hundred years, and likely joined the exodus.

Under David and Solomon, Judaism spread further. We recall that many Romans and Greeks converted in the last two centuries B.C.E. Those who are of "Jewish background", as we say, hail from many lands.

The practice of Judaism, today, is shared among cultures the world over; in Africa, Asia, and the Middle East, in North, Central, and South America, in Australia, throughout Europe, the United Kingdom, and Scandinavia, by people of all walks of life, and all regions of the globe.

Through different languages and dialects, ethnic traditions, and regional customs, Shabbos is observed, the words of Moses retold, and an ancient text, passed through millennia, is relived.

Judaism is an idea, a system of justice, a shared memory of common experience, and an age-old dialogue between humans and God. Above all, it is a faith, a sturdy pillar of wisdom, nourishment, and guidance that stands uneroded against the winds of time.

We are the Jews, we who walk in the steps of Abraham, a man from Ur, who crossed the Euphrates River four thousand years ago. We are the children of his children, of Isaac, Jacob, Joseph and Judah, followers of Moses and Joshua, David and Solomon, Prophets and Pharisees, Talmudists and Maccabees.

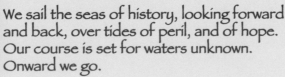

We believe in one singular, indivisible, invisible, Almighty God.

We sail the seas of history, looking forward and back, over tides of peril, and of hope. Our course is set for waters unknown. Onward we go.

4-10

do